Thomas Fletcher McGrew

The bantam fowl

A description of all standard breeds and varieties of bantams

Thomas Fletcher McGrew

The bantam fowl
A description of all standard breeds and varieties of bantams

ISBN/EAN: 9783337145804

Printed in Europe, USA, Canada, Australia, Japan

Cover: Foto ©Andreas Hilbeck / pixelio.de

More available books at **www.hansebooks.com**

THE BANTAM FOWL.

A DESCRIPTION OF ALL STANDARD BREEDS AND
VARIETIES OF BANTAMS.

FULLY ILLUSTRATED.

BY T. F. McGREW,
NEW YORK CITY.

PRICE FIFTY CENTS.

PUBLISHED BY THE RELIABLE POULTRY JOURNAL PUBLISHING CO.,
QUINCY, ILLINOIS, U. S. A.

INTRODUCTION.

BANTAMS have gained a position in the fancy far beyond the wildest hopes of their most ardent admirers. Only a few years ago they were spoken of as "Banties," and those who fostered them were considered a little off the regular line of the poultry fraternity; to-day they have the attention of the poultry world, and the most successful breeders in the land pay them tribute. In England, Canada and the United States the most accomplished breeders are using their utmost endeavor to produce some one or more kinds of these miniature fowls of a surprising quality, so as to astonish their fellow fanciers and gain prominence in the Bantam Kingdom.

In 1816 Moubray devoted to Bantams only thirteen lines of his book on domestic poultry; to-day, if alive, Burnham could write a book on the Bantam craze. Forty-five years ago Messrs. Wingfield and Johnson spoke of seven varieties, all that were known at that time; to-day we have over forty kinds and colors, all fine in form and plumage.

So much has been said and written within the last few years about Bantams that it would be quite impossible to say much of them that has not been previously stated. In compiling this volume, the author has gone through many books, written letters of inquiry to fanciers all over the world, and talked with every one known to him who knew aught of the subject. Facts thus obtained, together with those of his own personal knowledge, are herein recorded for the benefit of the reader.

It is the author's wish to present this subject not in a lengthy, scientific manner, but in a short, concise way that may be both attractive to the amateur and interesting to the matured fancier. Should this desire be fulfilled he will be fully compensated for the many hours spent in search and preparation of the data contained herein.

T. F. McGREW.

1899

THE BANTAM FOWL.

CHAPTER I.

THE proper housing of Bantams is the first and most important point for consideration. Almost any place will do for them, provided it is reasonably warm in cold weather, and free from dampness at all times. These little fowls have the constitution to stand very cold weather, but dampness is their almost certain destroyer.

From the time Bantams are hatched till the end of their natural life they should be protected from wet and damp. If this is done and they are properly fed, they will enjoy perfect health and repay you for all the attention they have received.

Young Bantams, when hatched, should be kept within doors on a dry board floor with the mother hen for about forty-eight hours, then removed into dry quarters outside and housed in a properly constructed coop with board floor that should be strewn with hay seed or chaff, or hay cut quite small. For my own use I have constructed a coop after the style of one made by Spratt's Patent. This is not all important, for any well constructed coop will do for their comfort, if warm and dry. We advocate very strongly the use of coops with board floors; at the same time, many advocate placing them in /\ coops right on the ground. Having used both, we cast our vote in favor of the coop with board floor well covered with dry litter, believing a greater number of just as healthy chicks will be raised in this way in all kinds of weather, and in a wet season, like the summer of 1897, the per cent is largely in favor of the dry floors.

FIG. 1.—POULTRY HOUSE WITH RUN UNDERNEATH.

For adult Bantams we also advocate houses with board floors, and we prefer these houses to be set at least ten inches from the ground, and so constructed that no vermin of any kind can make their home beneath the house. The illustration of our favorite style of coop for adult Bantams (See Fig. 1) will indicate our notion as to same. We also copy one from Spratt's illustrations, having added some of our own ideas to it. From our illustrations many forms of Bantam houses can be constructed; no matter how rude or cheap in form, just so they are dry and furnish protection from the very cold weather. Do not think for a moment that we would intimate that Bantams should be kept in warm or heated quarters during cold weather. They are quite hardy and withstand cold weather wonderfully well, but they should have comfortable houses to thrive and do their best.

For perches nothing is better than oval strips of wood, two and one-half to three inches wide on the flat side. Some say smaller perches are best. Try both and see which your fowls will prefer. Nest boxes and other furnishings you can select, as best suits your fancy. We use small pine boxes and find them very handy for removing with a broody hen to some quiet corner where she can bring out her brood in comfort.

Many of the finest exhibition Bantams of England are bred in very contracted quarters. We have seen a pen of five Bantams housed and yarded in a space less than seven feet square for a period of four months, and they produced a fine lot of healthy chicks, many of which found their way to the show pens and won their share of prizes. Quite a number of the New York prize winners are bred in very small city lots, where all green food and grit of all kinds must be furnished them. The secret of success in these cases is the great care bestowed upon the fowls. The most perfect sanitary conditions must be observed, and cleanliness must be the absolute rule of the hour. To occasionally clean up will not do. If kept in these confined, small quarters, they must be kept as thoroughly clean as your own house, for in this way only can they be successfully raised in confined quarters.

FIG. 2.—MADE OUT OF A DRY GOODS BOX. This makes an excellent home for a few fowls.

We breed our finest specimens in a small back yard, and use for housing a small wooden packing box, as shown in Fig. 2. Their run is about eight feet square, and they are turned out on the grass plot each day for a run. The two hens in one of these runs laid over one hundred and fifty eggs in four months, producing a number of very fine chicks, all of which were kept till eight weeks old, in a small door yard. After this age we sent them to a farm to shift for themselves.

Bantams should be sheltered from sun, wind, rain and snow by day, and from drafts by night. Shade of some kind should be provided for all Bantams intended for exhibition, for their plumage is soon injured by the hot rays of the sun. White turns yellow and black turns brown when exposed for days to the hot sunlight. We have seen the careful breeder spread sheets of canvas for shade when deprived of natural shade, for his fowls. These little pointers show what care the expert bestows upon his prospective prize winners.

FOOD AND FEEDING.

Bantams must be well fed, properly fed and not overfed nor underfed. Do not starve your breeding stock, but keep them in good condition and feed them on the proper amount of egg-forming food. Always give them the best, for they eat so little that what they do eat should be fine in quality. If fed morning and evening during the breeding season it is quite enough, providing attention is paid to quality and the proper quantity.

FIG. 3.—POULTRY HOUSE WITH COVERED RUN.

If confined in runs, plenty of green food and grit must be given them. When so confined, a meal at noon adds much to their comfort and condition. For green food, cut grass, clover, apples, beets, turnips, and the tops of almost any vegetable are good for them. This green food should be given at noon.

The best grain for Bantams is wheat, rice, oatmeal and some broken corn. When young it is best to cook the food for them. Boiled rice, mixed with corn bread, wheat bread, or a mixture of ground oats, corn and middlings made into a cake and baked is very good. Feed the chicks quite often, on small amounts each time. In this way they will not be forced to overgrowth. After weaning time a small feed of wheat

Fig. 4.—For Bantams, 3x6 inches, covered run for chicks, separate apartment for hen; drop door in front for chicks to go in and out; apartment for bantam hen, 12x2.

twice a day is quite enough for them if they have their liberty, where they can find seeds and bugs for themselves.

All Bantams should have some kind of animal food. If confined feed them a limited amount of ground green bone with some meat in it, not too much, and cut very fine. Cooked meat of all kinds is good for them, and there is nothing better than cooked fish. There are quite a number of prepared animal foods, many of them very good. The best of them is Crissel and Liverine. A mixture of Liverine, oatmeal and middlings cooked or scalded and fed warm and crumbling is a good occasional food. Crissel is excellent for laying hens. It can be fed in the same manner and is a fine egg-producing food. Grit of some kind, ground shell, bone and charcoal should always be provided in liberal quantities. They are great promoters of good health. After the breeding season, cut down the food ration of your old birds, only feed them as you do the young, growing stock, but when the cooler weather comes treat them as you do yourself, to a little larger allowance. One of the most important factors of success is plenty of pure, fresh water. This should be kept in some good style of fountain, protected from the sun in hot weather. These fountains should be kept as clean as your own cups and saucers, and fresh water should be provided at least once, and when very warm, not less than twice a day. The hen must quench her thirst and also consume enough water to furnish a large per cent of water in the eggs she lays. The better the

Fig. 5.—Built of rough lumber, 3x4 feet, movable open run, drop lid to close up wet or cold nights; ventilator above drop. Coop should be made with board floor. Make run as large as possible to suit convenience and space.

water supply and the food, the better she will lay. Here are a few hints on feeding young chicks. If you want bone, like in the Game Bantam, feed bone-forming food; if a short leg and plenty of feather, like the Cochin Bantams, feed rice and wheat. Always feed them the kind of food that has the tendency to advance the features most desired.

SIZE AND WEIGHT

We advocate that all Bantams shall weigh about one-fifth as much as the standard fowls they miniature; if less, so much the better. The smaller the better, providing they possess all the variety characteristics. We have seen them too small for Bantams. This is quite as bad as too large. The happy medium of size combined with the perfect form is most to be desired.

MATING

From three to five hens are quite enough for one male. Grade this according to his vigor and success in filling the eggs. Sebrights and Japanese do best in trios, and most of the other males do better with two or three females. Mate them early so they may become acquainted before the breeding season, otherwise their habit of quarreling when strange to one another may give you many infertile eggs. Do not hesitate to inbreed good, healthy stock, but do not make it a rule to mate brother and sister together. This is the most unlikely mating one can have. Father with daughter, or son with mother will bring improvement; also, cousins in line or to ancestors, but do not look for marked improvement from brother and sister, it does not work well that way.

Fig. 6.—Grand for winter and early spring. Should be built of inch boards and stripped. Coop 5x6 feet, run about same size and covered with glass to keep out wet and snow. The coop should have light and ventilation enough, so hen and chicks can stay in the coop in very bad weather.

BEST TIME FOR HATCHING

Bantams should be about six months old for males, and a little less for females before they are fully ready to show under the most favorable circumstances. We have won in strong competition with Bantam males five months old, but considered the specimen rather immature. By taking this as a guide you can hatch any time from April till August, and later if prepared to care for late chicks. Late hatched Bantams do well if properly housed; if not, they drop by the wayside and die.

CARE AND MANAGEMENT OF BANTAMS

The following circular came to hand with no name signed to it, but we consider it worthy of a place in our book:

"May and June are the best months to hatch Bantams. April, July and August are not bad, and September is all right if you have an extra nice place to keep the chicks in during winter.

"You can set the eggs under Bantams or large hens. A large hen that will sit on her own eggs without breaking them can do the same with Bantam eggs, as they do not break any easier than ordinary eggs. The only objection to using large hens as mothers is that they are apt to kill a great many chicks by stepping on them.

"In the care of the chicks the most important thing is to keep them absolutely free from lice. Remember the lice on

Bantams are the same size as those that infest ordinary chickens, therefore the Bantams will succumb sooner than the ordinary chicks. I use the utmost precaution against lice, but if I find a brood is not doing well I examine them carefully for lice. If I find any I dust them with insect powder; if I do not find any I dust them just the same. It takes sharp eyes to discover lice, but with experience you will be able to tell when your chicks are lousy by their general appearance.

FOOD AND WATER.

"Keep *clean* water before your chicks all the time, also plenty of grit, and for the first week or two finely broken egg shells, and after that oyster shells. Give all food dry. Bread crumbs make an excellent food for the first two weeks. Oats, wheat and corn are my principal standbys.

"Oats I use in the form of oatmeal. This is just the right size for the first few days. Then I give cracked wheat, and as soon as they will eat it, finely cracked corn. By the end of the third week they can usually eat whole wheat. I depend upon these three grains all through the growth of the chick, simply using the different forms to accommodate the size of the chick.

"A newly hatched Bantam will swallow only a very small particle. Give finely chopped, cooked meat twice a week. See that they have an abundance of green food all the time, and the more bugs and worms the better. Vary your diet as much as possible by using waste from the table, but be sure to feed everything dry. Wet or even moist food comes next to lice on the list of chicken destroyers. Feed five or six times a day at regular intervals for the first week or two, after that gradually lessen the number of feeds until by the time they are fully feathered two or three times a day will be found quite sufficient.

Fig. 7.—Double open coop for older chicks, 6x8 feet, making two apartments, 4x6 feet. This coop will house about 100 growing chicks.

A WRONG IDEA.

"There is a common idea that Bantam chicks must be starved to keep them small. If you wish even a moderate amount of success in raising them give up this idea at once. Until they are fully feathered feed them just as if you expected to make roasters of them. After they are feathered you may let up a little, but keep them growing, and when you pick one up it should feel plump and not as if its breastbone would cut through the skin.

"By this method you will undoubtedly get some overgrown birds, while by starving them you will get a great many worthless and misnarked ones, and the best you will get will not be equal to the best obtained in the other way, in either plumage, shape or vigor. Keep your Bantams small by selecting the smallest to breed from, and keep them healthy by good care and enough to eat. Nothing has done more to hurt the popularity of the Bantam than this idea that it must be starved to keep it down to standard size.

"Keep your chickens free from lice, give them clean, dry quarters, dry food in abundance, and you have the three main props in raising Bantams."

CHAPTER II.

THE GAME BANTAM.

THE most popular of all Bantam fowls is the Game Bantam. No variety of fowls is more widely known than the Black Red Game Bantam, and we must conclude, judging from the quality we find at some of our exhibitions, none so little understood. How often we see them of the same fashion as a young duckling, short of leg, long and plump of body, the female being shaped more like a pigeon than a game fowl, proving the lack of knowledge as to the requirements of a true Game Bantam.

First we will say a few words as to their early ancestors. More ancient than poultry lore is the game fowl. Of my own experience I can say that a personal friend who visited Pompeii saw a large flagon that had been taken from the ruins, on one side of which was engraved a game cock, on the other a peafowl, showing that fowls of this kind were known at that early day. Early writers tell us of Game Bantams, but we have only seen one record that places the credit of their origin. Mr. Entwisle, in his book on Bantams, states as follows: "We think we shall be quite within the mark in saying that not one of those we have placed in the intermediate class, such as Games, Cuckoo or Scotch Greys, Frizzled, Rumpless, Japanese and Buff Pekin, was known in England fifty years ago, certainly not sixty years ago." To Mr. John Crosland, of Wakefield, he gives the credit of having produced the earliest Game Bantams. In the few lines given to Bantams by Moubray (1816) he states: "There has been lately obtained a variety of Bantams extremely small and as smooth legged as a game fowl."

Mr. Hewitt, in writing of them in 1852, tells of a pair of Duckwing Game Bantams, which he describes as a beautiful pair. At the same time he mentions Black Breasted Red Game Bantams, a fac-simile of the game fowl, but not exceeding three-quarters of a pound in weight. He goes further and states as his opinion that the Game Bantam, properly so called, may be fairly considered as occupying a distinct place in the family. He does not give the credit of their production to any one, but claims for them the right of belonging to a distinct family.

Mr. Tegetmeier, in his book (1867), in writing of Game Bantams, tells of a Mr. Monsey, of Norwich, who produced them by inbreeding and selecting, also by crossing them on other Bantams. Neither of these gentlemen gives the credit of their origin to any one person. We simply present these records without comment to show the opinion of both early and modern writers as to their origin.

The Game Bantam, of whatever variety, should conform to the one standard for shape. Never be content with an off-shaped bird, no matter how good the color, for without the true Game Bantam form, color and markings go for naught. Never hope for good results in breeding from ill-shaped birds with poor carriage, for your reward will be disappointment. The main features are good style, hard plumage (that is, short, small and close-fitting to the body), small size and color. These, in the order named, constitute the true Game Bantam.

By style we refer to all terms used by experts and others not so well informed, such as carriage, symmetry, station, etc. The general style includes the shape of the bird and its ability to carry itself in the proper Game Bantam manner, and when this requirement is lacking the true Game Bantam feature is gone and the bird is of no value either as a show bird or producer of same. Much improvement can be made in some birds by training, but true style cannot be trained into a bird that is lacking in proper form.

The bird should be tall, upright and bold; the head long and narrow; the beak finely formed, long and tapering and slightly curved; eyes bright and clear, and face bright red, except gipsy face in Brown Reds; and the skin of the face very thin and close fitting. One feature of great importance and beauty is a thin, clean throat. When bred so fine that the female scarcely shows any wattles, the thin, clean throat adds much to the beauty of head and neck in both males and females. To show how long ago the absence of wattles was bred for, we state for your benefit, that the Black Sumatra Game in perfection scarcely shows any wattles. Our standard does not class them as Games, but they are of that same nature of fowls.

The neck should be long, thin and tapering from body to head, the neck hackle short and close fitting. The feathers of the hackle should not come together in front and they should end where the neck and back join. The shoulders should be broad, square and carried forward, and the neck should join the back and body between the shoulders, the prominence of which gives the appearance of the neck being set into the body. This feature is more prominent in the male. The back is short, flat and tapering, giving the body almost the shape of an egg; in fact, the body should be egg-shaped, and the wings should set very close to the body and be carried well up to the back. The end of the wings should not extend beyond the body, nor should any part of the wing drop or extend over the back. The shorter they are the better, and the higher the better, just so they do not cover the back.

The tail should be short, small and close, but slightly elevated. The tails of both male and female should be formed much alike, the male having a few short narrow sickle feathers. What is called a "whip tail" is most desirable. The breast should be neat, round and plump. We do not admire the flat breast on either Games or Game Bantams, nor do we advocate over-feeding till the crop becomes extended, which spoils the bird's appearance. They should be fed enough to fill out their breasts to their proper form, and not so underfed as to cause the shoulders to look narrow and spoil the whole appearance. The sides and wings should be round, not flat. In fact, the whole formation of the body should be round and tapering towards the stern; the whole body coming to a point, similar to the small end of an egg.

The legs and feet are of great importance. The thighs should be long, muscular and set well apart; in fact, well to the outside of the body. They should taper to the hock joint, which should be strong at the juncture with the shank, which should be long, clean and slender, almost round, and covered with small, close-fitting scales perfectly smooth and free from imperfections of any kind. The feet and toes must be sound and perfect in form, the toes perfectly straight, well spread and of good length. The hind toe should be set low and flat on the ground, and should be perfectly straight out behind, and not curved, crooked nor carried high. When the hind toes twist or turn forward, it is a grave fault, and a bird with this weakness should neither be shown nor used as a breeder, because this defect disqualifies for all uses.

Size is a most important feature and should be obtained by proper mating, not by underfeeding, for underfed birds can neither mature good bodies nor feathers. Always remember, style and size come largely from the female and, color from

THE BANTAM FOWL.

the male. Never use an overgrown female Bantam to produce small stock, nor a bad colored male for good color. Have both as near the proper requirements as possible.

The female should in all the above features conform to the male. Her shape and general form should be the same, with the few exceptions of tail, comb and head, but always of a more delicate or effeminate character. In the consideration of size, we hold it is just as bad to have them too small or undersized as to have them oversized unless their vigor and stamina can be retained. When too small their ability to reproduce is more likely to be dwarfed and their constitutional vigor impaired. No fowl of any kind is valuable when these facts combine to destroy its real use. The proper size of a Game Bantam is to be just as small as possible and yet retain all the characteristics of the game fowl. We have seen female Game Bantams that weighed under ten ounces. They are simply a novelty in the fowl line and should be classed with cage birds, for they are of little useful value. We think sixteen ounces is, under all conditions, about as small as a mature male bird has been bred and at the same time maintained all the features of a true Game Bantam, having proper vigor and endurance.

We recognize in our American Standard the following varieties: Black Breasted Red, Brown Red, Golden Duckwing, Silver Duckwing, Red Pyle, Birchen, White and Black. In addition to these there are the Malay, Indian Game and Aseel Bantams. The Bantams allowed by our standard must conform in shape to the description given above. As to color and markings, all must be treated separately. In doing this we shall present the views of the best breeders of both this country and England.

BLACK BREASTED RED GAME BANTAMS.

The face, top of head when trimmed, and throat should be a rich healthy red on the cock bird; beak, dark horn color preferred; eyes red; head, neck, hackle and saddle should all be of one shade whether orange or light red. We prefer what is called an orange, bright and pure in color and perfectly clear from any sign of stripe or markings. Of whatever color, it should be pure and true. A light red shading into orange is a bad defect in color for the show pen (but for pullet breeding, most desirable). The back should be a clear, pure red of a slightly darker shade than the neck. No better description can be given for the wing coloring than is found in the Standard of Perfection, which should be studied by all who hope to breed these fowls to perfection. The shoulder should be black up to the meeting of the back coloring which extends down under the wings; wing fronts, black; wing bow, bright red, or crimson as it is called in England. The wing coverts should form a glossy black bar across the wing; primaries black, the outer web of the lower feathers bay in color; part of the outer web of secondaries bay; balance of feathers black. Breast up to throat, body, stern, thighs, and tail black; sickles and tail coverts, lustrous black; shanks and feet, willow colored, of a greenish rather than a yellowish shade, and very smooth and free from all defects.

The female to be a perfect show color according to the fashion of the day, must show a shade of color not strictly as described in our present standard. We say the ground color should be golden brown penciled with grayish brown; the English say, one even shade of light brownish drab finely penciled with black. The English fashion of color is winning favor with our best judges. Our description is not a perfect description of the color as accepted by experts. The comb of the female should be small, neat and perfectly upright, in color red; wattles and ear-lobes very small, if almost none is perceptible, so much the better, but they must not be trimmed; red in color. The color of the head should conform to body color. If the body color is dark the head may be of a darkish shade; but one even color of head and neck is preferable and that should be golden with a narrow black stripe through the middle of the feather. The beak should be a dark horn color.

Back, wing-bows and coverts should be one even shade of brown, finely penciled with lighter brown; breast, light salmon, shading into lighter color toward the thighs; primaries, black or darkish brown; tail, black or dark brown, the two upper feathers powdered with the same color as back; thighs, light brown, and shanks willow. The above would describe a

FIG. 8.—BLACK BREASTED RED GAME BANTAMS.

standard female as per our standard. We should prefer a female of a little different shading (for we think it more like the bird that wins the admiration of both judge and expert), as follows:

The general body color very even and regular in markings, of a color rather on a golden brown shade, finely penciled with dark brown or black; throat, light salmon; breast, a reddish salmon, shading into an ashy color under the legs. The whole color should be very even, pure and free from any dark or blotchy shadings. This we consider a beautiful combination for a show bird. Such a bird is most valuable as a breeder.

To breed show birds of high quality is an art that can only be learned by experience. A few general points can be told, and when followed, success may be the result; but the production of high-class specimens is the result of study and patience. For the production of males, a perfect show male mated to Wheatens, or females showing a reddish cast on the wings, or females from a Wheaton mated to an exhibition male, is the best for good results. The best of all is regularly bred females from Wheaton hens by the best exhibition males. If once you can establish such blood lines of your own, you can hope for males of the highest order, but till then look for only a small percent of high-class males.

For females, the best results come from males of one even color of red all over. If the hackle and saddle shade into orange, so much the better. Such males, with the truest colored females, produce the best pullets.

BROWN RED GAME BANTAMS.

The face, comb, wattles and ear-lobes of both male and female should be dark purple. The male should be colored as follows: The portions of the body that are red in the Black Red male should be lemon colored in the Brown Red male. All other portions should be black, with a narrow lacing of lemon on the breast feathers. The shaft of the feathers that are laced should be of a pale lemon color, shanks and feet quite dark in color. Head and neck feathers should have a narrow stripe of black. All lemon colored feathers should have a light

FIG. 9.—BROWN RED GAME BANTAMS.

colored shaft, and saddle should be striped with black, same as neck feathers.

The female should have a golden or lemon color for head, running a little lighter for neck, which should be penciled with a narrow stripe of black down the middle of each feather; the balance of the plumage should be a lustrous black, the breast feathers laced with lemon. All feathers showing the lemon lacing should be laced with the same shade as the neck feathers. Whatever shade the neck is, the breast lacing should be the same, and each feather on breast of both male and female should be evenly laced all round with a narrow edge of the same shade as neck color. The legs and feet of both male and female should be quite dark in color. If black legs can be had they are by far the best.

Good colored Brown Reds bred together should produce both males and females of the proper color. To keep the color true the highest grade males should be bred to the most perfect females, and to regain any lost color in males breed from females that show good lacing on back and wing bows. Never discard a female that is well laced on back and wings, for she is of great value to improve the color of males. Cockerels that show too light color on back often make the best cock birds, having a tendency to grow darker each year. A true colored young bird is often too dark as a two-year-old. Some use Golden Duckwing blood to improve the color, but it is far better to use females as above mentioned, and thus save much trouble for years to come.

BIRCHEN GAME BANTAMS.

Birchen Games are the same in markings as the Brown Reds, only their markings are silvery white. For this reason we advance the opinion that the coloring of the Brown Reds should be more of a golden color; one after the Golden Duckwing, the other after the Silver, believing the lemon, or straw color, in fact, too faded a color to breed true and sustain itself as it should. We present below a description of this variety from the pen of Mr. S. Walker Anderson (Hon. Sec., pro tem of the United Game Club), of Scrooby, Bawtry, England, one of the most successful fanciers of the day:

"This new and pretty variety of Bantams has only recently come to the front. 1896 was the first year that classes for it were provided at the Crystal Palace, although they have been shown successfully in the variety classes. As yet we have no recognized standard. I have drawn up a standard giving the most points for that which every breeder will acknowledge to be the most difficult to obtain. The Birchen, as most breeders know, is a made breed, obtained by crossing a Duckwing with a Brown Red. You obtain a Birchen in the first cross, and many times might breed a specimen equal to many years' careful breeding with Birchen and Birchen.

HOW TO SELECT BIRDS FOR FIRST CROSS.

"You must select a Silver Duckwing cock with heavily ticked breast and streaky hackle, good black thighs and fluff; small in tail; very free from shaftiness or lacing. Of course it is understood that the birds must be of good shape, long head with plenty of reach. The Brown Red hen must have a good black face and eye, evenly laced breast, and light lemon hackle. And be careful that she has a clear cap. Body should be by no means shafty. From your first season's result select those nearer to the Birchen standard for next year's breeding stock, and in no case, however good, breed from a cock or hen that has a red face and light eye.

HOW TO SELECT BIRDS FOR SHOW AND STUD.

"You must first have a good shaped cock with plenty of

FIG. 10.—MR. S. WALKER ANDERSON'S BIRCHEN GAMES.

reach and style, long head and neck; face and eye as dark as possible; the beak, legs and toe nails black or very dark slate color; the cap, neck and saddle hackle silvery white (not creamy), each feather having a narrow black center. The breast, which is one of the most attractive parts of the bird, should be black, each feather having a narrow margin of white completely round it and the shaft of the feather faint white. I myself have a strong objection to a heavily laced bird. The thigh and fluff should be black. This point I consider most difficult to obtain as most cocks are laced both on the thighs

FIG. 11.—BIRCHEN GAME BANTAMS.

and fluff. The shoulder points should be black, saddle and beak a silvery white with a black center; bows and wings black; tail black, small and fine in sickle and free from shaftiness or lacing. The hen should have a good black face and eye. Cap and neck hackle are the same as male bird, also the breast; the rest of the body a glossy black. Legs, feet and toe nails same as the cock.

"General remarks: To keep Birchens in show form you must not expose them to the sun; if you do they will turn a straw color. I should advise keeping them in covered runs during the show season. Always destroy any brown-red chickens that are Birchen bred, if not you will never obtain a pure strain.

SUGGESTED STANDARD.

COCK.		HEN.	
Good head and neck	5	Good head and neck	5
Eye and face	10	Eye and face	10
Shape and style	10	Shape and style	10
Legs and feet	8	Legs and feet	8
Condition	10	Condition	10
Hardness of feather	8	Hardness of feather	8
Tail	10	Tail	10
Breast lacing	10	Breast lacing	10
Clear thighs	8	Clear cap	8
Soundness of color	10	Soundness of color	10
Size	10	Size	10
	100		100

DISQUALIFICATIONS.

"Duckfoot, crooked breast, deformed back, wry tail, light eye, red face, and straw colored hackle, saddle and back."

DUCKWING BANTAMS.

Duckwings are of most beautiful color when in perfection. The rich coloring of neck, back and wings forms a beautiful contrast to the bright, glossy black body of the males. Our standard for these fowls differs somewhat from the English in the point of describing color. In Golden Duckwings, head and hackle with us are straw color, the English standard calls for creamy white. The back in our standard is golden, with them orange or yellow. They prefer a creamy white hackle with orange back and wingbow. We call for a straw colored hackle and golden back and wing-bow with saddle same color as hackle, both of which must be free from any penciling or dark stripes. Of whatever color, it must be clear and pure, and free from any discoloration. The general coloring of the bird is the same as to markings as the Black Red. The wing bay of a Duckwing is of great importance. This is a weak point in most of them and should be watched with care in breeding. The shanks of both male and female, to look the best, should be a light willow.

The female in her make up follows the Black Red, having the salmon breast. Her back and wings are a slate gray; hackle silvery gray with a narrow stripe; body and stern light ashy gray, tail black with top feathers powdered with gray. Our standard omits the penciling in plumage of Duckwing females, but they should be penciled on back and wings, very fine and evenly, with black or dark brown." The head coloring of the Duck-

FIG. 12.—DUCKWING GAME BANTAM COCK.

wing should be very clear and pure, and the hackle quite free from any off shading.

The Silver Duckwing is a counterpart of the Golden, except in color. The male is a silvery white in hackle, back, saddle and wings, and the female is of a much lighter shade of gray, with a light salmon breast. A perfect Duckwing female is the most beautiful of all Game Bantam females when of perfect form and color. No Game Bantam is harder to produce in perfection than the Duckwing. They must be crossed with the Black Reds to keep up the color of the males, and this must be done in an understanding way or bad results will follow. Do not select them as a breed easy to handle, for they are a work of art from the hand of an artist who has well in hand the blood lines of his different matings. Do not be surprised if the progeny of a well selected pen of Duckwings disappoint you. It is quite essential to know their breeding to handle them for best results.

FIG. 13.—PAIR OF DUCKWING BANTAMS.

RED PYLE BANTAMS.

The Pyle Game Bantam cock, when bred to the true type of form and color, is one of the most beautiful of all Game Bantam males, and many assert he is the most beautiful. He is red and white, as the Black Red is red and black. If the red is of a bright crimson, and the white a pure, clear white, the combination is most attractive. Yellow legs and beak are most essential to a perfect make-up. Bad or off-coloring of any kind is quite objectionable, and while dark markings are not a disqualification they detract from the beauty of the bird.

The female should be pure white, with a golden hackle centered with white, and a salmon throat and breast, the color shading into white on thighs and belly; the purer and clearer these colors, the better. The breast color should not be of a reddish brown, but salmon of a red shade of color. The tendency of the female is to run light in color when produced from Pyle matings. This can be improved in many ways, but the better way for general purposes is to breed from

FIG. 14.—RED PYLE GAME BANTAMS.

females quite dark on breast and with red markings on wings. These birds show the strength of color as derived from the Black Red cross, and will improve color without so much injury to the leg color. But to produce and maintain a strain of high-class Pyles one must certainly feed into their veins some Black Red blood. This should come from a male with yellow legs and as pure and even a color as possible. Many rules for breeding these birds are given, but the safest and surest way is to use the most perfect males of the deepest red shade, with females having too much color for your cockerels, and with almost white females for your pullets. This will secure a general average of quality and many good birds of both sexes. When the color fails, introduce new blood as above mentioned and use the product of the cross to improve color.

WHITE AND BLACK.

Some very fine White Game Bantams with dark legs, sports from Brown Reds and Birchens, make their appearance. If these were bred to the White Game Bantams with yellow beaks and legs, a fine line of well stationed birds could be produced. The White Game should be pure white in color, with yellow legs and beak. They originally came from the Brown Red Bantams, as did the Black Games; both have the same common ancestry. The Blacks should be pure, lustrous black, with black legs and dark purple face, beak dark horn or black, eyes black or dark brown. These two varieties could be made most attractive if attention were paid to them.

OTHER VARIETIES.

THE MALAY BANTAM

Is a perfect Malay in form and color, almost as small as Game Bantams and of the following colors, White, Pyle, Black Red

FIG. 15.—A MALAY BANTAM HEN.

and Pheasant. Having described the other colors for regular Game Bantams, it is only necessary to tell of the Pheasant color: Comb, face, throat, ear-lobes and wattles, red; eyes pearl or yellow; beak yellow or horn color; head and hackle black; beak and saddle mixed dark maroon and black; wing-bows dark maroon; secondaries, outer web bay, inner web black; tail glossy black; balance of plumage black; legs and

FIG. 16.—PAIR OF WHITE ASEEL BANTAMS.

feet yellow. The female is just like an Indian Game female of high quality that has double lacing. Single lacing is admissible, but the other is preferred.

ASEEL BANTAMS

Are of all colors, such as White, Black, Black Red, Gray and Spangled. They are fashioned very much after the Malay type. Their necks are strong and muscular; legs short; plumage hard and short; thighs very strong and rather scantily feathered. Male weighs about two pounds. The female should resemble the male. Ear-lobes and wattles on both should be very small; back quite straight; carriage upright.

INDIAN GAME BANTAMS

Are just like the Indian Games, Laced and White.

THE PYLE WHEATON HEN

Has a very bright eye and a golden hackle; breast pale fawn at times almost cream colored; thighs and upper part of body light buff or lemon color; back and wings the color of wheat; primaries white; secondaries, outer web wheaton, inner web white; tail white, upper feathers edged with wheaton color, legs and feet are often light willow, but yellow is preferred.

THE DUCKWING WHEATON HEN

Differs from the above as follows: Hackle and head color is white, or white slightly striped with black; breast light fawn; back and wings pale cinnamon; primaries black; tail and legs same as a Red Wheaton.

RED WHEATON HENS

Have a red face, red ear-lobes and wattles, horn colored beak, golden hackle, fawn or cream colored breast, light buff thighs and upper part of body; back and wings pale cinnamon or wheat color. From this they get their name. Primaries black; secondaries, outer web wheaton, inner web black; tail black, upper feathers produced with wheaton color; legs and feet willow color.

BLACK BREASTED RED GAME BANTAMS

The following notes from Mr. B. C. Thornton, of South Vineland, New Jersey, will be of interest to all, coming as they do from one who has ability in handling Game Bantams. He writes: "In mating Black Breasted Red Game Bantams for the production of exhibition specimens it is best to use double matings, one for cockerel breeding, the other for pullet breeding.

"For cockerel breeding one should have a bright colored male bird, bright red or light orange hackle to top of head; one shade of color from top of head to end of hackle. Same color for saddle hackle, deeper color on back and wing, good solid glossy black breast, and good color on wing bay.

"The female should be a bright, light partridge color on back. A trifle of soft, ruddy color on wing is no objection, but not bricky red. She should have a light salmon breast, a bright lemon hackle, free or nearly so, of striping.

"For pullet breeding use a male of same color as for breeding males, provided you have very sound colored females perfectly clear of the slightest ruddy cast on side of wing. This mating will produce the bright colored females so much admired in this country, but somewhat lighter in color than is fancied in England. If possible, it would be best to secure a strain of birds noted for breeding each sex and mate them up accordingly.

RED PYLE GAME BANTAMS

"Are the most beautiful in color of all Game Bantams when

FIG. 17.—BLACK RED BANTAM MALE.

true to color. Not more than thirty to forty per cent of sound colored birds are generally obtained from the best matings.

FIG. 18.—RED PYLE GAME BANTAM HEN.

The rich color must be kept up with a cross of Black Breasted Red blood, and that is very apt to bring smoky white or yellow where there should be clear white, and it takes a long time to breed it out. My plan would be to breed two yards of these also, as, in fact, you will have to do with all varieties of Game Bantams to get a large per cent of really high class exhibition cockerels and pullets.

"In mating for cockerel breeding I should use a good, sound colored male bird with good, sound colored wings, rich crimson on back and wing coverts or wing-bow, and good color in wing bay or what is known as the diamond; white breast clear of lacing, good white on wing butts and wing bar, showing the markings on wing very distinctly.

"Females for this mating should have a nice salmon breast, fine golden hackle (a trifle rosy on wing will not hurt), the balance of bird a good white, not smoky.

"In breeding for pullets the cock bird need not be so rich in color, but the wing bay or flight coverts should be deep bay color, and all the white should be as clear white as obtainable. The females should have good salmon breasts, nice lemon or straw colored hackles, and be perfectly clear white, free from yellow, smoky or stone color on back, wings and tail.

BROWN RED GAME BANTAMS

"Are fast gaining ground with American fanciers, and some of the best from the other side are being transferred to the yards of American Game Bantam breeders. The fashionable color of to-day in the male bird is the bright lemon hackle and saddle, and as near to that color as possible on back and wing-bow; fine, narrow lacing on breast, coming well down to the thigh; body color and tail hard, glossy black.

"The female, in body and tail should be short, hard-feathered, glossy black in color, narrow, fine lacing of lemon on breast; hackle feathers black, deeply laced with lemon.

"In breeding for males I would use a male of the above description with good, hard-feathered female; if slightly laced on back it is no objection. They should be well laced on breast.

"For pullet breeding I would use only sound colored females, with lustrous black body color, no lacing except on breast. A slightly darker male than above described would be better for pullet breeding.

GOLDEN DUCKWING GAME BANTAMS

"Originally were the result of breeding a Black Breasted Red cock to Silver Duckwing females. They are now bred as a distinct strain and reproduce very true to name and color. A very bright colored Black Breasted Red male is sometimes used to secure good color in cockerels. Females from this cross are generally Black Breasted Red in color, and are only valuable when mated to true colored Duckwing males to improve the color.

SILVER DUCKWING GAME BANTAMS

"Were the old-time birds. They are bred extensively in America, but little in England. They are really a handsome bird when of a pure silvery white; much more beautiful than the Golden. No Game Bantam is more beautiful than a fine Silver Duckwing, and a female of this variety is the most beautiful of all Game Bantams."

CHAPTER III.

THE DIFFERENT VARIETIES.

UR present Standard recognizes fourteen varieties of Bantams other than Game. The English recognize some thirty odd varieties, including their many colors. We shall tell you all we can of these many kinds of Bantams, gleaning our information from English writers as to those we do not recognize in this country.

Our standard groups the Bantams other than Game, as follows: Sebrights, Rose Combed, Booted, Cochin, Japanese and Polish. We shall follow this order and continue the same by adding the many others not so well known.

Bantams were made, or reduced, from the larger standard birds of the same variety in many cases, but the original or early bantams came to us, whence, no one can tell. Some allot to India the credit of being the home of the first or original Bantams. Some also give the jungle fowl the credit of being the common ancestor of all of our fowls. Records show that poultry in Egypt was quite a feature ages before man began to record history. So great was the interest in those early days that Aristotle considered it of quite enough importance to tell of their mode of handling the artificial hatching of long years prior to his time. One could not imagine that much progress could have been made prior to this early day, and since his day the work could not have been in progress without the world knowing of it. Others would give to Java the honor of sending us the little Bantam, while others claim them as a product of crosses made from the Bankiva fowls of Java. This latter, when used as an attempted cross some sixty years ago, simply killed all other fowls placed with them.

CHAPTER IV.

SEBRIGHT BANTAMS.

Their Early Advent Produced Quite an Interest in Their Kind—Their Past Qualities Compared With the Present.

E hardly think Sir John contemplated the delight his production of Sebright Bantams would bring to the fanciers of the present time. No fowls are better known or more admired than the Sebright Bantam, and but few less understood. That most charming feature, clear, well-defined lacing, is so poorly understood or little appreciated by many, that it often makes one stop and wonder at the decision of experts who place the awards on them. The so-called Sebright of two pounds weight should be placed on the spit to delight the palate of an epicure, but never in the show pen or breeding yard as a representative of his kind. A good Sebright male should never go over twenty-four ounces, and a female not over twenty ounces, whether old or young.

In the fall of 1890, we wrote the following for *The American Fancier*, and consider it of value at this time:

Before me are two articles written by two of our most noted writers, judges and Bantam experts, the tone of which call my attention to the desired qualities of the Sebright and their shortcomings of the present day.

In the *Canadian Poultry Review* one of the above-mentioned articles, from the pen of Mr. Babcock, calls our attention to the color of legs on the Golden Sebright, and his statement I shall consider, for it covers a point so often advanced by myself, and which deserves careful attention. His statement is given in full below:

"The Golden Sebright has blue legs, and it looks very well with them, but did you ever see a Golden Sebright with greenish yellow legs? If you have you have seen a symphony in color, for then the legs harmonized with the plumage in a way which blue can not. I know that such legs disqualify the bird. I know that for the purposes of classification blue legs which are the correct thing on the Silver—are the best. But I also know that art is above standards and the rules of classification, and that an adherence to art would compel the Golden Sebright to have yellow legs. I do not expect to see this change made in the standard until the time comes when many other changes, based upon a compliance with correct taste, are made. When that time comes there will be many sweeping changes, especially in the color of legs, of the different breeds of fowls. In this respect the standard, while in harmony with market prejudices, is out of harmony with nature and the law of coloration. The result is that the best successes now obtained are obtained with great difficulty, and they are far from being what the second best could be under a differently designed standard."

These are very sweeping statements and worthy of consideration, and while I should join the writer in the statement that art is above standards, we must admit that the laws of nature are far above both. This being the case, yellow legs could not belong to the Golden Sebright for the following reasons:

First, their origin, their advancement and their completion and make-up forbid it. Second, yellow legs do not from natural causes belong to birds of their color.

As to the first we must consider origin, and on this point the best evidence gives us two very positive points. One, the female used in the start was a very small buff colored Bantam with clear slate colored legs, no doubt a Nankin. Polish was also used, no doubt the Golden; also a cock of a reddish color and a small hen resembling a Golden Hamburg. Three of the four we know had blue legs, and we can feel almost certain that the reddish colored cock must have had the dark legs of

FIG. 19.—PAIR OF GOLDEN SEBRIGHT BANTAMS.

the early Games, the majority of which had blue or olive legs. The only cross used that would indicate a yellow color of legs was the white bird used to produce the silver colored birds. The origin being so positive in the leg color, the product had it well stamped in the blood, and being the natural color of the original before the hand of man began to work changes of form and color, it claimed supremacy and held it.

As to their advancement, the club formed for their advancement about 1820 and continued for over seventy years, always mentioned in their requirements very specially the color of the legs. They say legs and feet are required to be blue. And this point being so positively established a change of color would be so radical it must destroy the color of the whole bird. When one so well informed on these points advocates so positive a change what must we think of a standard that allows in White Booted Bantams white or yellow legs when the special character of this variety is their white beak and legs? All white varieties if desired to be pure white in color will naturally in time have white legs and beaks. This again proves the superiority of nature over art or standard demands. Mr. Babcock also makes the following statements:

"It is not always easy to get the wings of the Golden Sebright just right. White will creep into the yellow and black will disappear from where it is wanted. Outside of the comb there is hardly a point where the breeding is so unsatisfactory as in the primaries of the Golden Sebright. Just why this should be the weak spot I have never seen explained and I have no explanation to offer. It may, perhaps, always remain one of the mysteries of breeding, and there are many to all except the beginner—he understands more on the start than

FIG. 20.—PAIR OF SILVER SEBRIGHT BANTAMS.

he will when experience has sobered his enthusiasm and reduced the size of his head.

"Another difficulty in breeding the Sebright is to secure narrow lacings which go clear around the web of the feather. The tendency is, if the lacings are narrow, to stop before they get clear around the web, and if they go clear around they are usually too wide and obscure the ground color and thus injure the beauty of the bird. My experience leads me to believe that this difficulty is greater in Goldens than in Silvers; why, I do not know—it is another mystery."

Here is presented the experience and opinion of one of our foremost experts about a breed of fowls now in its hundredth generation. He is compelled to admit the many shortcomings in the breed, one of our most artistic productions in fowls. Could the hand of man guide them still farther and produce the yellow legs and bold even as good qualities of color and penciling, or will nature refuse to lend her aid and thus destroy the whole? We all know full well how the attempts to govern the color of ear-lobes failed. How, then, can we hope for the yellow legs?

Many trials must be made before one can fully understand the troubles that confront us when breeding these beauties. Here are pointed out the hard, rough places to be found when trying to produce the high grade specimen required for the keenest competition. In a well written article in *The American Fancier* by "Zim," he makes the following statements:

"All of us know full well that a perfectly clear tail, a perfectly clear wing or a faultless comb are very, very desirable, yet neither of these coveted qualities makes a bird, regardless of his style, shape, or lacing of other sections. *Real judgment* is the kind that makes note of all the good and all the poor qualities of a bird, and awards the ribbon to the best all-round specimen, regardless of the fact that there remains in the class a bird unnoticed that has one or two exceptionally good qualities, and several just as objectionable qualities. This applies to mating and breeding as well. The would-be breeder of Sebrights of to-day simply needs to start *right* by buying birds of the right sort and continuing to mate and breed on the same line, and he can not go far astray, as they breed remarkably true to-day."

After considering all these points the reader must remember that no variety of the whole number of standard varieties requires more perfection in every section than the Sebright, from the point of his beak to the ends of his toes. All must be perfection. This being the case, he who desires to produce the higher grade of perfection must study well his matings, for no variety looks better when fine in form, color and markings; none less attractive when inferior in these points.

The standard for Goldens calls for color of a rich golden yellow, each feather evenly and distinctly laced all around with a narrow edging of black. Please consider this for a moment. What is a rich golden yellow? Is it the color of a fresh chestnut shell or an old almond shell? Is not the color of many of our Goldens entirely too dark, as judged by the wording of the standard? Is the black stripe kept to the narrow line? The answer must be "No." The color of the Silver Sebright should be a silvery white, with the narrow edge of black. Remember, a silvery white, not a yellowish white, nor any kind of white other than the silvery white. These colors, when true and properly striped with the narrow edge of black, form a beautiful combination. The narrow edge gives a bright, gay appearance. A broad edge of black spoils the whole appearance of the bird. Next to bad color are a long back and a drooping breast. These faults should almost disqualify a bird. Why is it, when the standard speaks so plainly on the points of form and color, that so many win honors that scarcely fill a single requirement? Too much consideration can not be given to these

FIG. 21.—SILVER SEBRIGHT COCK.
A Model for Style, Size and Marking.

words in reference to the Sebrights, taken from an English journal, as follows:

"What has been lost and what gained in this particular variety? Probably birds are now to be found as accurately laced as ever, and the pure white ground color of some strains of Silvers has been an introduction of later breeders. But what has the sacrifice been? To begin with, we can remember

THE BANTAM FOWL.

Sebrights little more than half the size of the present exhibition birds. Truly, in Bantams this is a great retrogression. Then the characteristic hen-tail of the cocks is seldom now seen in anything like perfection. But more than all, the beautiful coxcombical Bantam carriage has been lost. Let any fancier with an eye for form look at the lanky, ungainly tucked-up creatures now often in a prize pen, and then read descriptions of Sebright carriage a quarter of a century ago, and his only rational conclusion will be that much has here been lost. What says Dixon, whose book was published in 1850? 'Here is a little whipper-snapper! His ample tail, from which sickle feathers are absent, is carried well over his back. His dependent wings nearly touch the ground. He is as upright as the stiffest drill sergeant, or more so, for he appears now and then as if he would fall backward like a horse that overrears himself.' What again, writes Mr. Hewitt in Tegetmeier's poultry book? 'In the carriage of these birds we find the very extreme of pride, vanity and self-importance. The feet are raised in walking much more than in any of the other Bantams, and planted again with the greatest deliberation and precision. When alarmed their deportment is most striking. The wings drop to the ground, not listlessly, but as if determined to make the most of their tiny proportions, while the head is thrown back and the tail raised, so that they nearly meet.' Other writers lay stress on the nervous motion of the Sebright cock, being almost like that of the Fantail pigeon. These descriptions are hardly that of the Sebright of 1896. A large field, it seems to us, is open for the improvement of the breed by intelligent fanciers in smallness and carriage."

Even in England they are alarmed at the backward step in this variety of Bantams. The most important feature of the Sebright and the one most neglected is form and carriage. The standard calls for a very short back and a full round breast carried prominently forward. The body should be compact, deep and short. On one very important point the standard is silent, namely, carriage. This is the one very important feature of their make-up, as Mr. Hewitt wrote many years ago: "They are the very extreme of pride, vanity and self-importance." Their carriage should be upright and striking, not drooped nor indolent. We see too many long, ill-formed, unattractive specimens to-day. They should be bred up to the following form and color: The Sebright should be valued as follows—First, size and carriage; second, color and marking, always demanding perfection of all four, for when either is wanting the combination is broken and the true beauty gone. The color should be for the Golden, a rich golden yellow; for Silvers, a true silvery white. Any other color should not be tolerated. Both should be distinctly laced all around each feather with a narrow stripe or edge of black. Remember that any other color is absolutely wrong and a wide edge or discoloration of any kind in ground color is despicable.

The first point, size or weight, as per our standard, is wrong. The bird should be smaller. As to carriage, it is almost lost. When have we seen such style as exhibited in the cut of the Silver cock? Let all take lessons from the illustration furnished with these articles and try to improve this most beautiful variety of Bantams.

Another important feature is often lost sight of, i. e., the shape of the feathers of Sebrights. They should be almost round, or quite so at the outer end; not oblong or tapering. The round feather when properly laced gives the right form of coloring. When long and tapering the center has the appearance of an oval white or golden stripe on the feathers. This is a very grave fault, in fact so bad that we can not advise the use of such a specimen under any condition.

Mating for best results is a matter of importance, and but one method can be followed with hope of success. Always

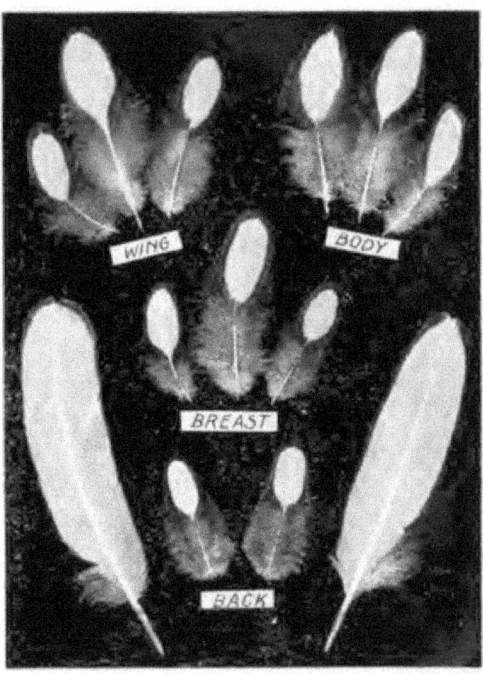

FIG. 22.—PHOTOGRAPHIC REPRODUCTIONS OF SILVER SEBRIGHT BANTAM FEATHERS.

use, if possible, hens over one year old for breeders. Whatever your females may be, have them small and perfect in color. If these females are light in the point of lacing, mate them with a male that is too heavy in lacing for the show pen. If the females are heavily laced, mate them to a light laced male. The tendency in this variety is to lose in color and lacing. Never hope for the best results from birds that are bad in color. None but the very best of this variety is good enough to produce fine specimens.

In regard to the male, study well the following: He should be sound of ground color; if golden, rather a little darker than the standard calls for, not on the reddish order, but like a fresh shelled almond; if silver, the ground color should be very clear, rather on the whitish order. Both should be evenly and plainly laced with a rich, greenish black. No mossy, smutty color of any kind ought to be allowed, and we must

THE BANTAM FOWL.

never hope for good results if much is present. Select one with this style of coloring and as little bad color as possible.

Get the very best wing, comb and tail you can find with the above color, and even then remember your selection is only half made, for you must have with this, perfect form and carriage, and small size. Always remember that twenty-eight-ounce birds are not likely to produce sixteen-ounce young stock. Two females with one male is better than four. If you use a cock bird over two years old, give him but one young hen. Always select birds with short, round feathers, and not long and narrow. Look well to the style and carriage of both male and female.

FROM A PROMINENT BREEDER.

TAUNTON, MASSACHUSETTS.

Mr. T. F. McGrew:

About breeding Bantams, I do not know if I can impart the knowledge I may think I possess. I have my ideas, but seldom speak of them.

In Sebrights, to keep the size down is one thing, and a great thing for me. This I have done by selecting a small male, with a small leg and as good color and shape as I can get. In size I have never had any trouble when I confined myself to my own strain. When I have introduced new blood by importing or buying here I always have increased the size. Comb, I never had any trouble about. I take care of that as I do in my other breed. Shape, we all have lost in Sebrights. Twenty-five or thirty years ago they were a proud, strutting bird and very pretty. But now they are long-bodied, and the ear-lobes may be white or red. To me it is a great mistake; since they have lost shape and the white ear-lobes they have lost their attraction for me, and if it were not for the pleasure of trying to get them back, I would have given them up years ago. I used to practice hatching them in August and September to keep down the size, but in these days of comparison shows it does not seem to make much difference whether they are large or small. The lacing I do not think I ever worried much about. By mating the very best laced birds that will almost take care of itself. Sometimes I have been troubled with the main color being a little light, but care in mating will fix that. Too much black or snut in tail we often have, and then one must mate a cockerel too light in color. Like all other breeds, when you think only of one section of the bird, you are apt to lose in the others, as in the case of the Light Brahmas of to-day. We look to its hackle,

wing and white surface color, and shape must take care of itself. We all follow fads and fashions. Is it not so?

P. WILLIAMS

FROM A FANCIER.

Mr. Ira C. Keller furnished us the following notes on Sebrights. His success with this breed makes his statements most valuable.

PROSPECT, OHIO.

Mr. T. F. McGrew:

Possibly there is no breed of Bantams that has had so much attention among the fanciers as the Sebrights. It is right they should, for there certainly is no breed that approaches them in style and beauty. The narrow lacing shows to a great advantage, and so strikingly that at first sight they captivate the visitors at the shows. Breeding Sebrights in years past was very wearisome, but to-day they are so well and thoroughly bred that they breed a very large per cent of high-class birds. The fancy to-day demands a narrow lacing all over the bird. This is rather difficult to produce, but has been greatly improved during the past five years. In mating, to produce this narrow lacing, we select the most narrow laced birds we have that are full laced throughout, with other points good, and by doing this year after year the lacing can be produced very narrow.

Shape and form need looking after. Early hatched Sebrights usually grow too leggy, long-backed, etc. The best time to hatch them is from the 15th of May until the 1st of September. One can produce smaller size and better form by hatching during these months. Most American breeders feed Bantams too heavy and too rich food. The Sebright likes free range best. It will find nearly all the food needed for its growth. They like to rove over pasture lands, through woods and along weedy fence-rows. If given their liberty they are extremely prolific and will lay nearly the year through.

In feeding young Sebrights, we feed during the first two weeks bread crumbs and oat meal; then we change to a chopped food of one part corn meal, one part ground oats and one part bran scalded and mixed to a dry crumbling mass. For the rest of the day we feed cracked wheat and corn, and as soon as they will eat whole wheat we give it to them. They grow to maturity very rapidly; usually are crowing at six to eight weeks old. No more attractive bird can be kept around the house.

Sebrights are very profitable to breed for show purposes. Good specimens are always in great demand at good prices. We have bred them for over twenty-five years and have never had any trouble in disposing of all we raise.

IRA C. KELLER.

CHAPTER V.

ROSE COMB BANTAMS.

They Might Be Called Hamburg Bantams, As Well As We Call Others Cochins and Games What Others Say About Them.

THE Black Bantam is spoken of at so early a day that some contend that it was his imprudent crow that got St. Peter into trouble. Be this as it may, he and his companion, the White, began their career long before any one took enough notice of them to keep a record of their beginning. Black and White Bantams with rose and single combs, with and without feathered legs, are mentioned as existing centuries ago. Moubray mentions in 1816, the fact that some Bantams were lately obtained that were extremely small, having legs as smooth as Games. He also gives to India the credit of their origin. (The earliest illustrations of Black Bantams show the rose comb and smooth legs). Other writers claim Java as the original home of all Bantams, but be this as it may, they came to England over two hundred years ago, and the original were booted or feathered legged. Of these we will write later, only mentioning the above facts to show about the date of mention of smooth legged Bantams.

The Black and White Rose Comb Bantams began to gain favor and prominence as show birds in 1850. About this time some were shown that only weighed as follows: Cock fourteen ounces, and hen twelve ounces at twenty-two months old. At this early day the Whites were very true to color. Then perfectly white plumage throughout without a single stain, could be seen. These birds had also white beaks, legs, toes and ear-lobes. Now we demand the yellow beak and legs and with them get the yellow plumage and ear-lobes, and for weight we allow twenty-six ounces for a cock bird, just twelve ounces more than the birds of fifty years ago.

It may be of interest to our readers to know what these Bantams were like fifty years ago, so we quote from the words of Messrs. Andrew, Gwynne and Bailey, noted fanciers of the time. As to weight, they say: "The less in reason the better, but never diminutiveness at the sacrifice of shape, feather and condition. The Blacks: The males should have a full crimson rose comb, with wattles and face of the same hue, but with ear-lobes perfectly white; plumage glossy black, reflecting purple tints; tail full and sickled; short legs, which with the feet should be of a dark horn color. The hen is dusky black, with her comb and wattles small, and of a dull leaden hue."

Of their appearance they say: "Bold of carriage, a very caricature of Bantam arrogance. For the Whites the same form is demanded, and color as above stated." Rev. G. F. Hudson bred wonders of the White variety in those early days, and he wrote that yellow beaks and feet were quite an objection.

In breeding Black Rose Combs at this time the dull color of former days is not allowable in the female. It must be as in the male—lustrous black. To obtain this rich black with beetle green sheen in our females requires special breeding.

A rich, true colored male must be mated to dull colored females to produce the best colored males. These same males mated to rich colored females produce fine females, but the males will show red in hackle and saddle and on wings. Male birds so bred should be reserved for pullet breeding only. To get the very best results, you must make special matings for both males and females. In selecting breeding stock special attention must be given to the quality of comb on both male and females. Look well for good shape, spikes and peaks, for no

FIG. 23.—BLACK ROSE COMB BANTAM MALE.

matter how good otherwise, a bad comb kills the appearance. Do not encourage bad lobes by breeding from either a male or female having them, for no fault will grow faster with as little encouragement. Do not pen more than four females with the male; three is better. If these points are well looked after and your birds are right in form, carriage and color, quite a large per cent of good chicks should be the result of such matings. Separate mating is not required for the production of males or females in the Whites. If comb, ear-lobe, color and form qualities are right they should breed fine specimens, but we favor the white bill and legs, knowing as we do, that our standard prefers them yellow. Our experience tells us that these colors add or detract from the pureness of both plumage and ear-lobes. The yellow beak and legs have an influence over the color of both, and the color is much purer when the white leg is well established in the blood.

To Mr. E. Hutton the credit is largely due for the present

English type of Rose Comb Bantams. They are miniature Hamburgs in all their points. No doubt they were crossed with the Hamburgs to establish the form and color. Our standard allows blue or leaden blue for the legs of White Hamburgs, and yellow or white for the White Rose Comb Bantam. When white, a pinkish tinge on the back and between the scales is allowed. We consider this a mistake.

The proper weights for Rose Comb Bantams in good show form are about twenty ounces for a cock, eighteen for a hen,

FIG. 24.—WHITE ROSE COMB BANTAM HEN AND BLACK ROSE COMB BANTAM COCK.

and in proportion for young birds. Some ounces less than this adds to their beauty if good form and vigor are maintained. When you consider that our standard only makes two ounces all along the line between a Rose Comb or Sebright and a Buff Pekin, you must be surprised to know that the English standard calls for a weight in Cochin Bantams, of thirty-two to thirty-six ounces for males, twenty-eight to thirty-two ounces for females; for Sebright Bantams, twenty-two ounces for males and eighteen ounces for females; for Rose Combs, sixteen to twenty ounces for males, fourteen to seventeen ounces for females, while we allow for the Rose Combs, twenty-two to twenty-six ounces for males and twenty to twenty-two ounces for females, six ounces more for each than they, almost one-half pound over their weight, and even then some of our specimens crowd close to the overweight line.

Most certainly the weights for Sebrights and Rose Comb Bantams should be reduced somewhat in our standard, and the birds should be bred to them. Again, our standard calls for a very short back for Rose Comb males, the English for a moderately long one. When did you see a Rose Comb with a very short back, being fashioned after the Hamburg? Their backs favor their forms.

Many little points like these should be well considered by all Bantam fanciers. We formulate our standard oftentimes without due consideration for nature and thus word a description that if followed to the letter would change the real breed characteristics.

To breed Black Rose Comb Bantams at the present time, one must strive for a very lustrous beetle green shade of plumage in both male and female. Dull colors will not answer. To secure this shade of color, the very best colored specimens of both male and female should be mated together. If this method of mating produces reddish shading in males, use dull colored females to reduce the brilliancy in the males and keep the females of this cross for producing males.

To secure pure white color in White Rose Comb Bantams use only as breeders birds that have pure white plumage to the skin, white quills to their feathers, white ear-lobes and whitish colored beaks and legs. If pure white in plumage and ear-lobes they can stand a cut for beak and legs if these are not the best of color.

CHAPTER VI.

BOOTED BANTAMS.

The Original or First Bantams Known or Recorded as One of Our Domestic Fowls Were Booted.

HERE the original Booted Bantam came from will never be known positively, but we do know that they came to us from Bantam, a town and district in Java, more than three hundred years ago, and that they were booted and of many colors, some having single, others rose, or double combs, as then called. How they came to that province never will be known. One of the early writers of 1850 tells us that feather legged and feather footed Bantams were among the earliest and most common of their race, and they were in color, black, white and yellow, and spangled in these colors. They were larger than now, and the feathers on their legs and feet were frequently four or five inches long.

Booted Bantams of the present day, like other fowls, are much improved. More varieties or colors of them are seen than formerly. Judging from the illustrations taken from Mr. Entwisle's book on Bantams, the shape would point to a cross with the Japanese Bantam. The back, neck and tail of the female, and the whole body and tail of the male, show the Japanese form on heavily booted legs. Either our Booted Bantams are behind the times, or the illustration is at fault.

The English recognize the following varieties in Booted Bantams: Black, White, Speckled Black and White, Speckled

than other Bantams, having been bred more for feather than for size, or, as some affirm, they have been allowed to breed anyway, with no definite set purpose in the mind of the breeder as to a model for perfection. The result is, some

FIG. 26.—BOOTED BANTAM FEMALE.
After the Japanese form.

closely resemble the Japanese in form and carriage, holding their wings and tail as they do, but having longer legs; others are shorter in leg and have a higher carriage of wing and a lower tail. This class finds more favor with our judges and breeders, and we think will continue to do so."

At the present time the English cultivate the Japanese form, only they wish the wings held up more and the tail thrown back or down more than the Japs, but they favor a shorter leg than formerly. On one point we should be very particular—the color of legs and beak. The white beak and legs are a distinguishing feature in them, as the pale bill is to the Aylesbury.

Booted Bantams should have a small, round head; bright, prominent eyes; handsomely shaped comb, and wattles of fine texture and rich color; ear-lobes, bright red and close fitting; neck, full or heavy at base, nicely tapered to the head and rather long as compared with the size of the bird; hackle, very long and flowing over back; back, short and rather slanting, the tendency towards erect carriage gives the back a slight incline towards the tail; body, plump and short. The wings, tail, hocks and toe feathering are the distinguishing feature of the Booted Bantams. These we shall try to describe as they should be in a perfect specimen.

FIG. 25.—BOOTED BANTAM MALE.
After the Japanese form.

Red, and Dutch Bearded. The Sultan Bantams are almost of the same class. The English writers place the Burmese and Silkies with them, but this, I think, is a little too much. I quote from Mr. Entwisle's book on Bantams, the following statement on Booted Bantams: "Take the best known varieties, White and Black Booted. Both are considerably larger

The wings of a Booted Bantam should be long in flights and carried drooping, not tucked up as in a Cochin. The hock feathers should be quite long; if five or six inches in length and quite full it adds much to the bird's appearance. Shanks should be long enough to properly support the feathering of hock, which should not drag on the ground; shank feathering not very full at hock, but should increase lower down. Feathers of outer toes and lower shank should be very profuse and long, the heavier and longer they are the more valuable. The heavy foot feathers, long wings and hock featherings of a fine specimen make it necessary to provide clean quarters for their home. When soiled and broken they are a disgusting sight.

The tail of both male and female should be full and car-

FIG. 27.— WHITE BOOTED BANTAM COCK AND BLACK BOOTED BANTAM HEN.

ried upright. The sickles of the male should be long and handsomely curved over the back. The tail should not be carried so far forward as on the Japanese, but a little after the Leghorn style of tail. The female is of the same form as the male, with much less comb, wattle, ear-lobe and hackle. Her hock and foot feathering should be very profuse.

The preceding describes the true form of a Booted Bantam in its natural condition, free from all taint of Cochin or Japanese blood. Of whatever color, they should have their own natural form and carriage. When fashioned after the White Cochin Bantams they should be discarded as of no value. The color should be pure silvery white; or, when of any other color, rich and bright of its kind. The Blacks should be rich and lustrous of color and their beaks and legs black. The Whiskered or Muffled are just like the others, only they have heavy muff or feathers on cheek and under their beaks, also shorter legs and not so much feathering on hock and feet. They are seldom seen. Only a few care for or keep them. The Splashed or Spangled are marked very much like the Houdans. Few fancy them and they are seldom seen, even in the show room. The Whiskered or Muffled Booted Bantams came from Germany to England about 1870. They had short legs, broad saddle and smaller tails than the other type. These were bred by a few who admired them in their purity. Some of very rich quality were shown by Mrs. Ricketts, winning in open competition against the others. These birds winning over the original type, changed the line of breeding somewhat; breeders adopted the shorter leg and higher carriage of wing. Many also adopted the Japanese form, with a longer leg, thus preventing the hock feathers from touching the ground. This intermixing of the heavy form and short legs of the Whiskered variety and the Japanese type has so changed the shape that you now seldom see good specimens of the original type in

White Booted. Why these changes should be made in form of these varieties we can not understand, while at the same time the winning Blacks are fashioned after the original style, having more size, the upright carriage, and legs long enough for the heavy hock featherings.

To reproduce the best form and feather in this variety select as your breeding birds the most perfect specimens. It is useless to hope to produce valuable young from inferior breeding stock. Poor specimens have no value. The only real merit in a Booted Bantam is superior quality. If this is lacking they are no better than half-breeds. The most perfect specimens obtainable yield but a limited number of really meritorious chicks. This being the case, discard all that fall below the line of real merit and by using only the best, improve their quality.

When the old birds begin to molt and the young to lose their chick feathers, great care should be taken to prevent their foot feathers from being broken. About six weeks prior to the time you wish to exhibit them they should be cooped in dry, clean quarters. Coops not much larger than an exhibition pen are best. This prevents their scratching and destroying foot feathers. The floor of the coop should be covered with dry sand and should be cleaned each day. Never allow any food to fall into the sand, as this tempts them to scratch. If any part of the plumage is soiled it should be washed properly before sending to the exhibition. See full directions in another chapter on "Washing for Exhibition."

SULTAN BANTAMS.

Sultan Bantams are so much like the Booted Bantams that

FIG. 28.—WHITE BOOTED BANTAMS.
Reproduced from "Poultry," England

we will put them in this class for description. The Sultan fowl is first mentioned in the Poultry Book of Tegetmeier as coming from Turkey in 1854. They are described as being the Sultan, or Feather Footed White Polish, resembling as they do the White Polish in many ways, having, however, shorter legs and fuller tail equipment, with vulture hocks and leg and toe feathering. They are somewhat smaller than the Polish fowls. The Sultan Bantams are a Sultan Booted Bantam, crossed and reduced by selection; or, in other words, a White Booted Bantam with a crest like a Polish and five toes like the Sultan.

Our standard recognizes only White Booted Bantams. The Sultan Bantam is not recognized by us. The White Booted Bantam could be made a most attractive variety if carefully bred. We should add the Black variety to our list.

In breeding these birds, mate together the most perfect specimens you can find, and reduce their size by selecting the smallest each year for breeders. Always use white birds that have white beaks and legs. Never tolerate in your breeding yards any other color than white beaks and white legs for White Booted Bantams, and you will soon establish this as a fixture in your birds. Decide whether you prefer the old style or original Booted Bantam or the new style fashioned after the Japanese form. When this question is decided, use only birds of the desired type.

BRAHMA BANTAMS.

These Bantams should be the counterpart of the standard Brahma fowls. The facts as to their production differ somewhat as they come to us from different sources. Some claim a cross with Brahma fowls and Japanese Bantams; others, an intermixture of Aseel and Cochin Bantams, while still others claim a direct Brahma cross with Cochin Bantams. If we desired to produce them, we should prefer to depend on the Brahma-Cochin Bantam cross. The Brahma Bantams, as we now have them, need to be improved in size and markings. Many of them have almost perfect Brahma shape. The Lights lack in the penciling of hackle, and the black in wings and tail. The Darks are good in color. The females lack in penciling. The Light Brahma Bantams of the present have fairly good Brahma combs, shape and body color. The under-color of most of them is white; the neck hackle of males striped more or less toward the lower edge, not much toward the upper part of neck; head very dark, wings only partially black, tails very good in color, and coverts of many of them are edged with white. The females show more and better color in both neck and wings. Some few of the females show a tendency toward dark or slate in under-color. All have good color of beak and legs and plenty of leg and toe feathering. With these qualities to start with it is quite unnecessary to consider how to produce them. The question is, how shall we improve them?

In selecting your breeding birds, have the darkest male you can secure in point of wing and under-color of back and shoulders. This will help to improve the white necks. If in addition to dark under-color you can have a fairly good neck, also tail coverts, much improvement can be hoped for if the females are fairly good in these points. Use the best colored females that it is possible to secure. Do not hesitate to use one very dark in under-color, for on this you must depend to build up your color by following these colors from year to year. Fine Brahma markings can be produced. The preceeding is our opinion as to the proper matings to improve color of neck, wings and tails. We also give the matings as recommended by Mr. W. F. Entwisle, to whom much credit for the production, is due:

"To breed good Light Brahma pullets, select as light colored a cockerel as possible, clear in body color and saddle, and only slightly striped in hackle, with the darkest hackled and blackest tailed hens possible to obtain, with white backs and wings. To breed cockerels, select the most perfect cock or cockerel you can obtain, good in hackle and saddle, very full feathered and fine in shape. Put the bird so selected with hens as white in wing and body as possible, even if a little wanting in color of hackle. These matings are not certain in their results, but there is no more reliable rule that can be followed by those of little experience."

This style of mating must produce nice, clear white birds, but can not improve the black markings so much desired by us.

Dark Brahma Bantams should be a perfect counterpart of larger fowls of the same kind. Those we have seen shall be our guide in describing them. The male bird is a perfect Dark Brahma in color, rather large for a Bantam and with too much tail for a Brahma. The top color is clear and silvery, and he is much better in neck than the Light Brahma. The body, in color, is fairly good as to the shade of black, but badly marked with spots of white. We have never seen one with a

FIG. 29.—LIGHT AND DARK BRAHMA BANTAMS.
Reproduced from "Feathered World," London.

pure black breast and fluff, but the comb, beak, legs and leg and toe feathering in both male and female are very good. The females are fair as to color; penciling very uneven and indistinct; tails oversized, and the birds themselves larger than the Light Brahma Bantams. To bring this variety within bounds calls for careful study in mating them.

Select the smallest specimens of both males and females which you can secure; use only females that show a tendency to penciling in their plumage, and males that are very clear in top color. If this mating shows improvement in the plumage of the female select the best of them to breed back to the sire, retaining some of the males to breed with the females of the next cross. In this way you can build up your blood lines. Never breed brother and sister together. By following this rule for three or four seasons good results must be the outcome. The Darks have better general markings to start with at the present time than the Lights. For this reason better results may be expected with them at an earlier day than with the others. Both will demand patience and proper handling to make them perfect Brahmas.

BUFF BRAHMA BANTAMS ARE AN AMERICAN PRODUCTION.

Below are the facts as given by Mr. F. A. Roppleye, of Farmers, N. Y.: He secured from Mr. Putnam, of West Sutton, Mass., some cross-bred Bantams, the result of a cross with Golden Sebrights and Buff Cochin Bantams, some of them almost perfect in Brahma markings. The best of these females he bred with one of his standard sized Buff Brahma males and produced fine specimens of about three pounds weight. These were crossed with some birds produced by crossing Sebrights, Japanese, Silkies and Buff Cochin Bantams. These crosses produced better Pea Combs and Brahma markings than the other. The offspring of these crosses have been improved by selecting the most perfect specimens and breeding them together until the proper size and marking for a Buff Brahma Bantam is his reward.

The following notes on Brahma Bantams have been furnished by Mr. Rowland Butterworth, Pownall Hall Estate,

FIG. 30.—DARK BRAHMA BANTAM COCK SULTAN.
Bred by Mr. Butterworth.

Wilmslow, Cheshire, England, who is now the leading authority on Brahma Bantams.

"Brahma Bantams are increasing in popularity with marked rapidity, and in consequence many of our leading shows have suffered considerably with some of the classes, for other varieties than games, as one of our leading papers has already stated.

"We have to thank the late Mr. W. F. Entwisle, of Wakefield, for their first introduction, which I believe was in the year 1885. Other strains have made their appearance, but I believe that he was the first to exhibit this variety. In manufacturing them, other breeds were introduced and it will be understood that this was a necessity. One could not expect to get a cross direct from a large Brahma and, say, a Pekin Bantam. Among these birds introduced were the Grey Aseel and the Booted Bantam. The latter I consider was a mistake and one that gives Brahma Bantam breeders considerable trouble to this day. Any breeder of the Booted Bantams will have noticed the great prepotency of this variety, with his legs close together, vulture hocked, and worse still, a space without feathers on the shanks just under the hock. I draw attention to this fact for the guidance of our new fanciers, as traces of this Booted Bantam blood appears in almost every hatch although the parents may not show any signs of these defects. It is also a curious thing that those defects are much more strongly marked in the cockerels than in the pullets.

"I did not commence to manufacture my strain of Dark Brahmas until 1884. The cockerel that I commenced with was one of a well known large strain. He was hatched late in the season and reared on foods heavy in flesh formers, but deficient in bone forming material. He was quite a great success and weighed six and one-half pounds when fully matured. The others from the same lot were much larger, coarse in bone and some nearly double his weight. I am not going to tell you what breed of hen I mated with him, but I managed to get eighteen chickens from the pair. The first season, I had not a single grey one amongst them, but there were two pullets excellent in shape, good foot feathers and excellent Brahma heads and combs. In color they were something like very bad colored Light Brahmas with a fair amount of brown in them. I mated these two with the six and one-half pound cock, and the next season every chick hatched was a good gray color, but only three showed much sign of penciling. However, with careful selection, always choosing the pullets with the finest bone, I managed to get one fit for exhibition in 1889. I was very proud of her. She weighed thirty-two ounces when in full feather. I won a first prize with her in a mixed class, the first time I exhibited her. I then had several successful seasons with this variety, and in 1893 I bred what I believe to be (and it was also the opinion of many of our best judges) the most perfect Dark Brahma Bantam ever exhibited, 'Pownall Pride.' An excellent portrait of this bird appears in 'Entwisle's Bantams,' drawn by our popular poultry artist, Mr. Ludlow. I still have this little bird and she is in the best possible health and weighs under 20 ounces now. Although a fat old hen she won 1st Crystal Palace and cup Fairfield in 1893, and a large number of prizes the following two seasons at our leading shows.

"The great difficulty in breeding Dark Brahma Bantams is to get hard feather, so many of the chickens coming soft and satiny, and such quality of feathers seldom carries much penciling. I say seldom, as I have had one or two specimens with this satiny surface that carried remarkable penciling, but it is the exception and not the rule, and such birds are not to be relied upon in the breeding pens. In breeding Brahma Bantams it is necessary to mate up separate pens for cockerels and pullets, and you can not expect first-class pullets however good in penciling your hens are, from a cock perfect in his breast and fluff, nor will you get good cockerels from a perfect colored cock and heavily laced hens. The mating is the same required in the larger varieties, with the exception that the neck and legs should be shorter in proportion than those accepted in the larger variety. This is most important, as it gives the Bantam "make-up" necessary for the show pens.

The Dark Brahma Bantam cock should have head feathers of good, clear white, distinctly striped with black, the stripes getting wider down to the shoulders and back. The back and wing-bow should be clear white, well striped with black, and the stripes increasing in width on the tail coverts. The breast, thigh, fluff, shank and foot feathers should be as black as possible. The tail is black, but a narrow white edge to the sickles is considered a point in their favor by many judges. The wing-butts and shoulders are black; wing-bars, tail coverts and side sickles, beetle green; shanks as yellow as possible, generally a dusky yellow; beak, horn-colored; comb, wattles and lobes, bright red; the comb small and triple; eyes, red. Hen, white on head and evenly striped with rich black on her hackle. The tail should be black, slightly marked with gray, the rest of the body one shade of slate gray, with a dark, almost black, pencilings. There are often other shades of gray in the winners, but the slate gray birds I find retain their colors longer than those with light ground color. The Brahma Bantam is quite distinct from the Cochin, and must be active, lively and spirited.

LIGHT BRAHMA BANTAMS.

"We owe this introduction into our poultry yards to the same source as the Darks, as they were manufactured at the same time, and I know of no other strain than the ones in England, although having been in the hands of various breeders for some years, who having different ideas as to what they should be, have changed them so much that they now look like distinct strains when they meet at the exhibitions. Light Brahma Bantams are much easier to breed than the Dark, although not so taking to the eye of many fanciers. They are certainly easier to meet with, as the Darks are now very scarce indeed. Light Brahma Bantams should be exact copies of their larger brothers and sisters in miniature, with the exception that they should be shorter in leg and neck. These points are of great importance, as they give the Bantam 'make-up' required.

"In mating for show cockerels a perfect colored show cockerel very sharp and dense in his hackle markings, mated with a hen very pure in her white and in hackle rather deficient in marking for the show pen, will breed what you require.

"For the production of show pullets you require a perfect colored hen very sharp and intensely black in her hackle striping, mated with a cockerel lightly striped in hackle and a good, clear white. If you follow this advice you will get both cockerels and pullets that are good, typical specimens in color.

"The Light Brahma Bantam cock should have a pure white head, a pure white hackle, the lower part distinctly striped with black, the breast, shoulders, wing, back and thighs pure white. The fluff is white, but often the under fluff is gray, and such specimens are very useful in the breeding pen when the hackles are growing weak in striping. The saddle is generally slightly striped but this should only be lightly marked, and not too much of it. The primaries and secondaries should show black on their inside when the wing is opened. The outer feathers of the tail should be slightly edged with white and it is in the bird's favor if the sickles are also laced with white. The toes, shanks and scales should be bright yellow or orange, also the beak.

"The hen should have a pure white head and very darkly striped hackle; breast, thighs, wings and body all pure white, the primaries and secondaries showing black, like the cock, the tail black, with white lacing or edging on the upper feathers. The strongest birds have always bright red eyes and are to be preferred to the yellow-eyed ones." R. B.

Just how to bring the Dark Brahma Bantams to the highest perfection of color and penciling is the most important point. They, like the Partridge Cochin Bantam, will be valued in proportion to their high qualities of color and fine finish of penciling. The fine gray color of the Dark Brahma female and the delicate dark penciling must be most perfect in these Bantams or else they are of no value. We lay before our readers the advice of experts who have shown their ability to successfully handle the large specimens. Below are the words of the time-honored Mr. Philander Williams, who donates his experience for our use.

TAUNTON, MASS., Sept. 24, 1897.

Mr. T. F. McGrew:

In regard to Dark Brahma Bantams, I would say, I know nothing. Of course, they are produced from a cross of some varieties and it is evident that they have not been bred long enough to have the color established. I see no way to get the color, but to breed them together and then select each year such specimens as you think will improve the color. I think the proper way to breed Dark Bantams is by a double mating and breeding in, although I never did this. The reason, I will tell you further on. I always have mated to breed nicely penciled pullets. I have always tried to have a nicely striped hackle and saddle on the male, but prefer him mottled considerably on breast and fluff. You will remember when the females were quite brown, but now you see quite often a nice silver gray hen with scarcely any brown, and I believe this has been brought about by light colored males and breeding in. I never have dared buy a male because I did not know his breeding, and unless you do know how a male was bred he probably would spoil the color of your females.

I give you a little experience. Last season I found my males had poor hackles and saddles, so much so that I was compelled to buy a male. I mated him, but you may be sure I had other matings of my old stock. I did not expect to get any well penciled pullets from the new cockerel and I was not disappointed. Cockerels are good, and an improvement, but the pullets are way off. Now, I do not care what the breeder says about the breeding of the cockerel, and I did not ask him a word. I know he was not bred out of nicely penciled females. But you take this cock (now) and mate him with nice shaped females with little or no penciling and you will get splendid cockerels. I said I never dared mate to breed cockerels, because they would be good for nothing as breeders and one might be tempted to breed them because they would be so handsome, and thus lose years in breeding penciling in females. I see no way for you to do only to breed the Dark Brahma Bantam and select each year the lightest colored cockerels and, what I call, *work them up*. You can do it, but it will take time. Partridge Cochins are the same as Dark Brahmas in breeding. PHILANDER WILLIAMS.

MORE ABOUT DARK BRAHMA BANTAMS.

WALTHAM, MASS., Sept. 24, 1897.

Mr. T. F. McGrew:

Yours of the 18th at hand, asking me how I would proceed to bring Dark Brahma Bantams to as fine color and markings as shown in my best specimens of standard Dark Brahmas. In reply I must say that I would never expect to accomplish that while at the same time I was trying to dwarf them in size to Bantams. I have had twenty years of experience in breeding Dark Brahmas exclusively. I have tried many experiments and made careful note of the successes and failures, not only my own, but those of others. Long ago I discovered that quite as much depends on the care and feeding, and locality where they are grown, as on the stock they are from. I have had birds raised in different localities, all from eggs from my very best hens, but to see them in the fall one would suppose them from as many different strains. Those raised on poor soil without plenty of shade, and perhaps poorly fed, would be a sorry lot, not one in a dozen that I would not be ashamed to have seen in my own yards; while another lot of the same age would have a fair amount of fine specimens.

Every year I have raised two or three dozen at home, where they have had the best care I could give them, and among these few I have always found my best birds. It seems strange, but it has always been my experience that whenever chicks are stunted they have invariably been bad in shape and worse in color. Hence I say I would never expect to get such color on birds that have been hatched very late and starved to make them small, as I would on birds encouraged from the egg to make strong, vigorous specimens. The same care and feed that make flesh make feathers. I have never raised a bird that was a cripple or stunted in size, that was good in plumage. If you succeed in establishing a strain of Dark Brahma Bantams that are as fine in color and markings as is often seen in the standard Dark Brahmas, you will have accomplished a great feat, and will be entitled to your reward. I appreciate your ambition. H. A. MANSFIELD.

DOUBLE MATING

NISKAYUNA, N. Y., Sept. 28, 1897.

Mr. T. F. McGrew:

In order to mate for pullets I take a mottled breasted cock or cockerel with hens or pullets. This cock must have a good silver hackle, good dark under-color, and no red in wings. For cocks I take a dark breasted cock or cockerel, silver hackle, good under-color, no red in wings and free from white feathers in the toes and legs when they can be so obtained. For pullets you want the hens rather dark. These are the points I use. Hoping this will do you some good, I remain,

Yours truly, JOHN H. WARNER.

PEKIN OR COCHIN BANTAMS.

The Five Varieties Considered—What Can be Made of Them.

The five varieties of Cochin Bantams are the most attractive of all Bantam breeds. Their beautiful form and colors, and hardy constitution make them the most desirable as a general purpose Bantam, giving them a commercial value, as well as fancy. They are very prolific layers of rich, high flavored eggs, and their plump little bodies make either a broiler or a pheasant, when needed for special occasions.

One of the marked differences is the deep or reddish color of the male as compared to the female Buff Cochin Bantam. This was the natural color as they came from China. The proper way to breed them to conform with their natural condition is red males to the lighter colored females. This kind of mating reproduced that of their kind.

The red color of the male should not be encouraged by preference; rather should a good, sound buff in both male and female have the favored place. If the standard would demand small size in all varieties, a pure buff, black, white, or partridge color, as it may be, with no foreign color in either, we would soon have all varieties conforming to one uniform standard for shape by adopting a proper form and holding to it. The size and weight of Pekins, as in all Bantams, should be about one-fifth of the size and weight of the large or standard breed of the same variety. We believe this is the English rule on all Bantams, and it might be a good rule for us to follow. Do not, however, for one moment fall into the grave error of thinking that the smaller the better for all Bantams. This has gone too far already with some varieties. All Bantams should be as small as the law of nature will allow and still maintain their form and vigor. When below this they should be discredited for undersize and loss of constitution.

Fig. 30.—Side view of Cochin Bantam Male.

Cochin Bantams are troubled with two grave faults, bad shaped backs, and too long legs. These faults seem to be more serious in the Buff than in the others.

We must not expect to remedy this in a year's time, but all should contend for better form, feathers and color.

The standard calls for the same general form as for standard Cochins, but it must be remembered that the tail formation of Pekins is quite different from their larger cousins; so this alone must change their form somewhat. Figures 30 and 31 show what might be considered proper form from side and rear views of the male.

To be good Cochin Bantams they must be miniatures of standard Cochins. The neck of the Pekin should be short and full, in fact, the neck of the cock bird should be very full and heavy looking, see Fig. 30. The back should widen from front to rear, saddle very full. The cushion and saddle of a good Pekin cock should rise from between his shoulders and not just forward of the tail proper, as is so often seen. The tail should be very full and surrounded with abundant saddle feathers and tail coverts with but few hard quills. The tail should help to add shape to both back and saddle. The fluff under the saddle and tail should be very full. This formation makes the most perfect and handsome looking bird. This is the natural tail formation for the Pekin, see Fig. 31.

Fig. 31.—Rear view of Male.

The legs of the Pekin should be short, in fact, a mature cock bird when well feathered, should appear as if his body almost touched the ground. To have this form his body must be set low between the legs, and the fluff must be quite abundant; this also widens out his legs and adds to their breadth. Always remember, however, that a Cochin Bantam never reaches its full form under sixteen or eighteen months, and is often two years old before it is fully developed. Quite often this is forgotten, and we expect to see a matured form on a young specimen.

The female must also conform to the description of a standard Cochin. Head, neck and body formation, should be a miniature Cochin. The divided back so often seen, more especially in Buffs, should be guarded against; this is from lack of cushion and a narrow tail. The narrow or flat tail grows up between the wings, unsupported by any cushion, and gives the divided form of back, which is the very worst defect a Cochin Bantam can have, and should be stamped out as soon as possible. Do not hope to do this in a day, for it may take years to fully accomplish it, as it did in the standard varieties, and even now it is often seen in them.

The cushion should begin just back of her shoulders and sweep back about the tail as in a well formed Cochin pullet of the larger variety. The Pekin's tail being composed of flexible or soft feathers adds much to the beauty of a proper back and cushion, see Fig. 32. The tendency at this time is to improve their form and color by crossing with the larger Cochins, and that is changing the tail formation to conform more to the larger Cochins.

Fig. 32 furnishes the rear view of the proper formation—broad, full and well feathered with good fluff almost to the ground. This is a description of a fully developed hen. Do not hope for this just yet in a pullet. Let it be your aim to produce this form and feather, if possible, on a pullet, but feel satisfied when you have it in a moderate degree, for the female, like the male, continues to improve in form and feather each year, and never fully develops until the second year.

The combs of many of our Cochin Bantams are much larger than their size and beauty demand. This might be improved, and also the shape of the comb. No reason can be advanced for a small Cochin cock having a comb almost as large as a Leghorn's. All these points only need our close attention to be soon corrected.

The following points should be always remembered in breeding Cochin Bantams: The neck should be short and full, neatly arched; the body should lean slightly forward, and the top of the tail be almost as high as the top of the head on the male. The head should not be held high above the body on a long, slim neck overlooking a slim, flat tail; all these points must be considered in the producing of a perfect Cochin Bantam.

Fig. 33.—Rear view of Hen

The Cochin Bantams came from Pekin, China, to England in 1860. The first that came were Buffs. For many years no other color was known, and then came the Blacks. At the time of the coming of the Blacks the original Buff stock was almost run out by inbreeding. They were improved by crossing them with White Booted Bantams. This cross aggravated

FIG. 34.—BUFF COCHIN BANTAMS.

the tendency toward extended hocks that still exists in this variety. These crosses produced the foundation of the Cuckoo Pekin stock, afterwards built up with birds of the same markings from China. The early Black Pekin males were crossed upon the Buffs, and this cross produced some cockerels very near Partridge color. The cross of the White Booted Bantams on the Buffs also gave the foundation for the Whites. We give our English brothers the credit of building up the five colors of Cochin Bantams. We of this side of the world have made several efforts to produce by crossing and reducing some Partridge Pekins, but up to this time nothing of much value has resulted from our efforts. Many have introduced standard Cochin blood into the Buff Pekins with some benefit. No one has, to our knowledge, produced either Partridge or Cuckoo colored birds of high quality in this country. Some are now being bred and we hope to see them in the show room.

BUFF COCHIN BANTAMS.

Buff Cochin Bantams, as stated by the best English authority, were first bred to some extent by Mr. Kenick, of Dorking, who bred in and in from the original importation for almost twenty years, until size and constitution were gone. Others secured some of the same stock from him and introduced new blood by importation and a cross, as above stated, with the White Booted, building up their constitution. Some also introduced Nankin Bantam blood. This cross did not harm the color of feather to any great extent, but it darkened their legs and made them longer, also reduced the leg and toe feathering and spoiled their shape and form of back, breast and tail. Evidently the first that came to this country were tainted with the Nankin blood, for a large per cent of them had bad colored legs and scant leg and toe feathering. Those produced here of good form are descendants of a cross with the standard Cochins and reduced by crossing with smaller specimens.

Mr. Entwisle of England, who purchased some stock from our country writes of them as follows: "One great point we value most highly, and we think our English breeders will not be long in recognizing, is the sound, even color insisted upon by the Americans. They say: 'A Buff must be a buff, perfectly free from any dark shade in fluff or fleece of feather, buff under the wing when expanded, buff in all the tail and foot feathers.' A bronze tail is considered a blemish, and the Americans do not allow such faults to be hidden or disguised by pulling out the faulty feathers." These words are quite complimentary to our ability to breed good color and should be strictly adhered to. If all judges will continue to refuse to place awards on coops containing specimens that plainly show evidence of being plucked, whether Bantams or any other kind of fowls, in a very short time none of this kind would appear, and all would buy or breed the right or standard forms and colors.

We will refer to a few points of difference between our standard and the English. Plumage of Cochin Bantams with them is so described: "Very abundant, long and quite soft; the fluff which grows between the saddle and thighs so full as to hide the latter; weight, thirty-two to thirty-six ounces." The cut of an English cock will illustrate this. This feather formation and full breast make them look very short of leg. Their demand for general shape and carriage is as follows: "Broad, deep, plump and well rounded; the carriage bold, rather forward, but low, the head being not much higher than

FIG. 35.—AN ENGLISH BUFF COCHIN COCK.

the tail." The weights are in the proportion demanded for all Bantams, one-fifth of the regular Cochin. This is the same in our standard for females, but for males we demand less weight than one-fifth.

Nature has declared for the Buff Cochin Bantams in their natural state that the males shall be of richer and darker color than the females. When mated, the females, if several shades lighter color than the male, will produce, females of their own color and males like the sire. A light colored male bred to females of his own color produces better males than females. The latter will be much paler of color than the mothers. This has been overcome somewhat by the cross with the large Cochins.

The color of the Buff Pekin, whether male or female, must be pure and true, whether of a light or dark shade. We began two years ago to work for the proper buff shade for both males and females, using a light colored male with a hen whose breast color was the same shade as the breast of the male. Two cockerels from this mating won first and second at New York in January, 1897. One of the same lot headed first pen at the same show. In getting this color we have lost some in the color of females, also in under-color of both male and female. This year, 1897, we have used these males on the best colored females and feel satisfied with the result, as the young stock shows much improvement, many of the males being an even golden buff throughout, and the females are much better than last season.

FIG. 30.—BLACK COCHIN BANTAMS.

BLACK COCHIN BANTAMS.

Black Cochin Bantams come next to the Buffs, and here we shall again quote from Mr. W. F. Entwisle, the noted English writer, whose words far exceed our ability in describing them. He writes as follows: "In Black Cochin Bantams, color of feather and brilliancy of sheen very properly count highly, quite as much so as color does in the Buffs. The desired color is one of uniform, lustrous beetle green, as seen in the Langshan and Black Hamburgs to the greatest perfection. The under fluff should be black down to the skin, but it is very rare that we can find a bird perfect in this respect. All the points of head, face, wattles and ear-lobes are the same as in all other Cochins, bright red, neat, smooth and even. The eye in the Black Cochin varies more than in any other variety, some being very dark brown. This we think as grave a fault as a white or pearl eye. We think the eye of the Black Cochin should be red. In breeding Blacks, it has often been noticed that it is very difficult to obtain the most perfectly colored cockerels and pullets from one pair of birds, the rule being that all the most brilliant colored pullets' brothers have more or less red feathers in their hackles, backs or saddles; whereas, all the soundest and best Black cockerels' sisters are wanting in luster or sheen, and look quite inferior in color to the pullets bred the other way.

"Where there is ample room for the purpose," Mr. Entwisle tells us, "even in starting from one common parentage, two distinct strains should be built up, the one for producing cockerels free from red or straw colored feathers, and using for this purpose only the deadest black pullets or hens mated with a sound black cock, and avoiding the more lustrous hens or pullets.

"And, on the other hand, we should select the most lustrous, beetle green winged and breasted cock, however much red he shows in neck, back or wing, and mate him with the most brilliantly colored hens or pullets, provided always that other essential points were sufficiently in evidence." (The writer has demonstrated to his own satisfaction that good colored males and females can be produced from the same matings when good colors only are used. With us in America, our motto is good color, surface and under-color. This rule, properly followed, the desired end will be gained.)

The proper handling of all Black fowls depends largely upon the true color of the male. If the male bird is a cock bird of true color the chances are that a large per cent of his chicks will be true to color. In selecting breeding stock of Black Cochin Bantams go down to the very skin in neck, back and breast feathers; also look well to color of wings at the very point where they come from the flesh. If the color is dark clear to the skin it can be depended upon. No strain of black fowls ever produced all of its chicks pure black. Some produce quite a large proportion of pure black females, but few produce true colored males, and those in turn produce but a small per cent that are perfect in color. This can be improved year by year if only cock birds of the truest color are used, for you can place dependence on the reproducing of true color if the sire himself is a two-year-old. The more of the bright lustrous sheen on your breeding stock the better. Even if they produce some offspring with red cast in plumage, it is far better to maintain the rich beetle green with a per cent of birds with reddish cast than to lose the color and have white. Both Black and White Cochin Bantams have a tendency to white in ear-lobes. This should be guarded against with great care. It usually comes with the very best specimens and the temptation to use them often overcomes our better judgment and stamps the fault upon the flock. It takes years to get rid of. Better keep it out than be compelled to breed it out.

We consider yellow legs a mistake on Black Cochin Bantams. If you have on your birds yellow legs and white in neck and ear-lobes, you may be certain the blood is bad and you need not hope for pure black in plumage. Better discard your whole flock and begin again with a few well selected birds from some well established strain that has perfect color of ear-lobe and plumage, with dark colored legs, the darker the better, just so they show yellow inside of feet. If we hope to establish a pure, solid black plumage, we must get rid of all the yellow possible in every part of the bird. They are not a utility fowl, so give them all the advantage possible in color.

As to the point of overcoming one fault by extra good points in the same section of the mate, this may counterbalance the fault, but you can depend upon it the fault will show itself in the future. Never breed from a bird with a serious fault in shape; get the best and discard bad defects.

CUCKOO COCHIN BANTAMS

Cuckoo Cochin Bantams are of late production, starting from sports of Blacks, Buffs and Whites bred together and strengthened by birds of the Cuckoo color imported from China. Never having seen any of this color, we give you a description of them as written by Mr. Entwisle, the greatest breeder of Bantams. He said:

"Cuckoo Cochin Bantams should have very sound orange yellow legs, and orange beaks are generally preferred, though personally we do not dislike a little dark marking on the beak of a Cuckoo Cochin Bantam, as it seems quite in harmony with the feathering. And now we must try to describe the color and markings of the Cuckoos. These points vary very considerably from a pale, almost white ground, with cloudy and indistinct markings, to a beautiful, soft French grey ground, with dark slate bars. The more clearly defined and the finer the markings the better. Not only does the ground color vary, as well as the color of the bars or markings of the feathers, but also in different birds the pattern of the markings varies considerably. There are Cuckoos shown with the same pattern of markings as the Dark Brahmas and Partridge Cochins—concentric circles of penciling, one with the other, i. e., in the hen—but this is not correct. The marking we require in Cuckoo Cochin Bantams is a series of clearly defined bars (we prefer narrow ones) across each feather, from the head down the hackle, breast, thighs, wings, back, saddle and tail, and, in fact, each feather throughout the whole bird, both cock and hen, must have this distinct barring, or series of bands, across the feathers. In some birds we have counted nine bars across the hackle or saddle feather of a cockerel, but seven bars make the feather look well. A less number would not be so good. In hens, across the saddle feathers, five bars are sufficient, and as feathers on other parts of the body are not so long, a proportionately less number of bars is required. The same description of marking is required on the feathering of the legs, feet and toes, and the more distinct the better.

"A common failing of Cuckoos is to have some of the wing feathers white, or with a good deal of white in them, and also in the tail feathers. This is a grave fault, and is reproduced in the chickens most persistently. If the fault is seen in the brood cock, it will not do to run hens with him having the same fault. If the cock bird is perfectly sound in color, less anxiety need be felt about a little white in the hens' flight feathers. Never breed from any—either cocks or hens—that are broad, coarse or irregular in their markings."

PARTRIDGE COCHIN BANTAMS.

The Partridge Cochin Bantam has the same standard colors and penciling as the larger specimens. They are the latest production in the Pekin variety. As stated, their origin was a cross of Buff and Black bred to large Cochins and reduced by care and patience to the proper form and size. The same method of producing males and females of proper colors in the large varieties must be followed with them. We hear of superb specimens of this variety being shown in England; but their idea of color of Partridge Cochins and ours differ so much that due allowance must be made in this line. The writer is now breeding a strain of Partridge Cochin Bantams that are small in size, fine in form, and very good in color and penciling. These birds show good length of feather and fluff, also fine foot feathers, and it is my belief that within a few years they will be fully the equal of the very best Cochin Bantams. This strain has its origin in English bred birds, crossed on a small standard female and recrossed on the imported stock. We can now feel assured of a good foundation in this variety. The winners at New York and Boston last winter were a sample of what the stock may be expected to produce. The same stock won over all others at both New York and Boston in 1898, proving their quality.

Past experience in breeding this variety has taught me the great importance of color in the male bird used to produce pullets. Of all the birds produced last season (1897) not one male bird had to be destroyed for lack of standard color. Many pullets were of no value, their color and penciling being so defective. To produce the proper color of female the deepest red possible to obtain in males is necessary. Having been produced with a Black Breasted Red Bantam cross, but few of the males formerly showed good penciling in hackle. This is improved by the cross with a standard or large Partridge Cochin female, and now both hackle and saddle show indications of the black stripe.

Another fault in this variety is the tendency to long beak, fashioned after the Game Bantams. Great attention must be paid to this, for it detracts from the Cochin form and beauty. The color of the female in these Bantams is not so rich a brown as it should be. It has a tendency toward a yellowish brown,

FIG. 37.—PARTRIDGE COCHIN BANTAMS.

and not a reddish or mahogany brown, as demanded by our standard for Partridge Cochin color. All these shortcomings must be improved by the careful mating of the best. They are to-day better in many ways than their larger cousins were ten years ago. They have fine Cochin shape, good leg and toe feathering and almost perfect color in the males. With these great advantages to start with, careful handling will soon reduce their size and perfect the color and marking of the female and make them fully the equal of any Cochin or Cochin Bantam.

WHITE COCHIN BANTAMS.

White Cochin Bantams of very good form and color are bred by a number of Bantam experts. They are quite well feathered, and as a class average better in general Cochin characteristics than the other varieties, the chief difficulty is the tendency of the males to turn yellow in color. This fault can be bred out of them by using as breeders birds having a perfectly white shaft in their feathers. This may have a tendency to whiten the color of leg and beak, but better this fault than yellow plumage.

It is said by experts, that the purest white specimens, when first hatched, show a sooty shade of color. This grayish color is said to promise better color when matured than the yellow cast. Of this we can not say from experience, but we know that if pure white to the skin when hatched, they will mature to a beautiful pearly white. The Whites, we believe, will become the banner Bantam of them all.

In many cases the White and Black specimens far excel the Buffs in true Cochin qualities. They, like all but the Buffs, came from a cross with their larger cousins and carry the Cochin shape, none but the Buffs having suffered in shape and feather by the cross with Nankin and White Booted Bantams. These faults are fast disappearing from the Buffs, and soon we may hope to see Cochin wonders in miniature form of the five colors at our exhibitions. Of one point too much can not be said. It is quite true that the smaller the better if true Cochin type is maintained, but close feathering is not Cochin form. Cochins should have long, fluffy feathers, and these close-feathered birds that look small should not be allowed to gain the ascendency, for if they do the true Cochin Bantam is gone.

The following is from the pen of Mr. A. P. Groves, a true fancier, who contributes his experience to this work:

CHESTNUT HILL, PHILADELPHIA, PENNSYLVANIA.

Mr. T. F. McGrew:

The American White Pekin or Cochin Bantams were originated by me about eight years ago. I was breeding Buff Pekins at that time and some of their progeny came pure white. I bred these white specimens together and established what is known as the Snow-Drop strain. There was no Booted Bantam or other blood used in their composition. They are

FIG. 38.—WHITE COCHIN BANTAMS.

now well distributed over the United States, and some have gone to England to compete for prizes there. In many instances they have been successful. I consider our home-bred birds the equal of those sent from England, if they are not the superior. Some of these may be whiter in plumage, they having paid more attention than we to this point, but in shape, leg and toe feathering we acknowledge no superiority. Having as careful breeders here as there are on the other side, why should we fall behind them?

I consider the White Cochin, when well bred, the handsomest of the Bantam family. Care should be exercised in breeding them. Only birds of good shape and heavy leg and toe feathering should be used; otherwise you will have many culls. Never breed from a bird with light leg or toe feathering, no matter how good otherwise. In regard to feeding the chicks, give them bread soaked in sweet milk, not too wet. for a month or six weeks; after that give them whole wheat. I have followed this rule for several years, and seldom lose a chick.   A. P. GROVES.

BLACK COCHIN BANTAMS.

Of all the breeders of Cochin Bantams none have surpassed Mr. David A. Nichols, of Monroe, Connecticut. To him is due the honor of establishing a strain of Black Cochin Bantams free from all white in plumage. The following is from his pen, especially for the readers of this book:

MONROE, CONNECTICUT.

Mr. T. F. McGrew:

I can not think myself a successful breeder of Bantams; each year brings me some new disappointment. Hopes cherished for months fall away in non-realization of some improvement confidently looked for. But still, many of these disappointments are softened with the knowledge that other points are strengthened and we are better and stronger for another season.

My first selection of Black Cochin Bantams was made from the best I could find. Color, form and size were not so good then as now. These I bred from and improved each year by selecting the best of all and inbreeding, always discarding a fault in form or color, till I had established a solid black plumage on some fairly well formed birds. These were mated to hold color and improve the Cochin form. The records must tell whether I have been successful in my efforts or not.

My chicks are hatched under hens on a farm near by (not having room at home), light-weight barn-yard fowls being used as sitters, each hen having from fifteen to eighteen eggs. Each hen is given from twelve to fifteen chicks to care for. They and the mother hen are placed in a coop out in the garden, or where no grass grows, as I have had poor success in my efforts to rear them on a grass plot. The birds, when young, will ramble in the grass when it is wet from rain or dew, and a few days of this will cause them to dwindle and die.

The chicks are fed the first few days on cooked oat meal. After one week they have the food known as H. O., and are fed with this till large enough to eat wheat. When at this age they are confined in covered wire runs and not allowed to roam about and grow too fast. I find that when allowed their freedom they are quite liable to grow into oversized birds.

The breeding birds are kept in separate pens that have a wire netting cover over them to prevent the birds from getting out or into the wrong pen. It also prevents hawks or cats from bothering them. It is quite a pleasure to see a hawk dart down for a specimen to his liking and injure himself on the wire covering. In pens of this kind you will always feel content that the birds are quite safe.

Upon the subject of mating I will be silent. Having heard the saying, "Tell a chopper by his chips," it is far better that I should not claim the art of knowing how to mate or produce good ones, for by so doing I lay myself open to the criticism of those who do know how.

D. A. NICHOLS.

CARE OF BANTAMS.

SPRINGFIELD, OHIO.

Mr. T. F. McGrew:

When the breeding season commences, move pens entirely away from the winter quarters. For houses use a common store box, make a slanting top, and cover all over with tar paper. Make south side a wire door. Runs should be covered with grass or sand and must have plenty of shade. If runs are large a good feed of wheat at night is a plenty; if small, some oats in morning and wheat at night should be given, with green bone three times a week and a trifle of corn once a week for a change. Do not let them get too fat. Incubators and brooders should not be used except where large numbers are raised. In early spring set hens in a warm, dry house by themselves. Make nests at least a foot off the ground. Later make nests on the ground. Be careful about sudden changes of food or weather, or bowel trouble will surely follow. When chicks hatch move the brood to a warm, dry shed with a sand floor. Sand should be changed two or three times a season. Keep the hens in coops, but let the chicks run in the shed. The first week I feed thoroughly cooked rice. Give fresh water three times a day and a nice green piece of sod each morning. After a week feed cracked corn, millet and rolled oats, a little green bone once a week, but not much as it causes bowel trouble. If chicks get dysentery or bowel trouble feed nothing but cracker crumbs and cut green catnip. There is nothing better than catnip to check the bowels. Wean when six weeks old and place in a shady run by themselves and feed wheat and corn, gradually reducing the food to two light meals a day.

Separate the sexes the first of September, and October first move back to the winter quarters, which have previously been thoroughly cleaned and the runs sown in wheat or rye. A large, well ventilated house is the thing for Bantams. Do not use a low, dark house.

In winter I feed wheat in the morning, millet and cut clover at noon, cracked corn at night, and green bone twice a week. I find a hot mash for Cochins or Cochin Bantams is not best in cold weather. They will eat it heartily, but after the temporary effects of the heated mash wear off they stand around and shiver and take cold easily. Commence in the morning and make them scratch all day. They will lay better and keep healthier. When Bantams are molting increase food and give a small quantity of flax seed and yellow mustard seed once a week. Do not fail to have a well filled dust box in each house the year through, and in summer spade up a place in the runs. Let them play in the dirt, that is, nice, fresh soil, not filth. It will help to keep them free from lice and their plumage in better shape.

To see what lice can do, I took two green legged chicks from a brood ten days old, that were apparently hearty and well. On the throat of one I placed three gray lice, and on the other, four. In two days the latter died, and in a little over three days the first one died. They were subjected to the same care and treatment as the rest of the brood, which have all lived. So you see too much stress can not be put on the lice question, especially with reference to Bantams. I prefer vaseline to any other grease for head lice, but prefer to use none if it can be avoided. Coal oil or lard kills chicks as well as the lice in a great many cases. Powdered moth balls, one part; snuff, two parts; insect powder, four parts, make the best insect powder I ever used. Two or three moth balls placed in the nest with the eggs will keep both hen and chicks, when hatched, free from lice. It is fine.

As to mating, I mate with these objects in view:

First, shape; second, color; third, size. Or first, a Cochin; second, a Buff Cochin; third, a Buff Cochin Bantam.

In the male I want as light surface color as possible, but must have a sound under-color, and I depend on him for comb, color and carriage. In the female I want a deep color (not brown), very good shape and feathering. Too much care can not be used in selecting the male. This is contrary to nature, and red will crop out strong in wing-bows of cockerels for a few seasons. Dark males and light females do not go with me. Do not discard a good shaped or colored Bantam because it is too large; nor breed a delicate, puny one because it is small. You are breeding trouble if you do. I believe it is all hosh about using a male with black in tail because it holds up color. The sooner Buff breeders drop that notion the quicker black will disappear in wings and tail. (The tail does not wag the bird.) Do not breed a green legged bird for a farm in Texas; white is bad enough. What we need, and need badly, are judges who know something about Bantams. Not one in ten pays any attention to long, straight, dark colored beaks, depressions in front of eyes, lack of depth of keel bone, long flight feathers, lacing of feathers on back of females, etc., and as long as the judges do not be the breeders will not. The successful breeder of to-day is the one who selects a variety best suited for his purpose, studies it carefully, uses an abundance of grit, patience and common sense, adapts himself to his circumstances and surroundings, and sticks as closely as possible to the lines of nature.

CLARENCE HENDERSON.

A BREEDER OF WHITE COCHINS.

ELBERON, NEW JERSEY.

Mr. T. F. McGrew:

We imported our first stock of White Cochin Bantams from England. We made altogether seven importations, and we can candidly say there is no necessity for going there except for new blood to prevent inbreeding. In fact, after the new standard is out we will not be able to import, because they breed them with both yellow and white legs and beaks. The best White Cochin Bantam we ever imported was "Nameless." She was undoubtedly the best White Cochin Bantam ever seen in America. She was even smaller than any pullet. When she was four years old she was sold for the longest price ever paid for a Cochin Bantam in this country. Messrs. Butterfield, Ball, Zimmer and Rockenstyre considered her perfection. The yellow legged strain was produced by a cross of the English and American White Cochin Bantam, breeding for a type with yellow legs and beaks, and by a very strong use of the ax on culls.

Feed bread, cracker crumbs, oat meal, grit and wheat, with this breed. Beware of yellow corn as you would a pestilence. Where one has plenty of shade one can produce that sheeny white plumage.
CHARLES JEHL.

SECRETARY NATIONAL BANTAM ASSOCIATION.

FLATBUSH, LONG ISLAND.

Mr. T. F. McGrew:

I do not think I can give you anything of particular interest regarding the handling of Bantams, as you requested, but will send you a part, at least, of my experience.

I generally mate three or four females with one male and have several matings. The eggs are saved from the middle of April and chicks are hatched during the first week of May. When young I put the chicks in barrels at night, with the opening facing toward the south. These I find are satisfactory, as they shed the rains and afford a dry place for the broods. I put a quantity of earth on the bottom and pack some up around the outside, always placing the barrels on higher ground than that immediately around them. I lay a board over the front, which furnishes a shelter from showers and breaks any hard wind. When the hen leaves her brood I change the chicks to dry-goods boxes about four feet square. These I tilt about one foot back by nailing legs on the front of the box, and place three or four roosts inside. A slight cover partly over the front keeps the rain out and gives a proper shelter to the stock. By the use of plenty of kerosene no trouble is had from lice at any time of the year. The stock is allowed to run over a tract of land, not being confined until nearly matured. Bantams require a change of food and must be fed when young or the chances are that not many will survive. I give raw beef quite often and all the grain they require. They are easily cared for if they receive the proper start in the spring.

E. J. LATHAM, Sec'y Nat'l Bantam Ass'n.

CHAPTER VII.

JAPANESE BANTAMS.

The Manner of the Japanese in Producing Birds, Plants, Trees and Flowers.

THIS house, time is not considered by the Japanese when producing or improving a plant or flower. Consider the patience and time consumed to produce the many varieties of form and color in chrysanthemums. We can to-day surpass them in fine colors and forms, but this is only our ability to make use of the productions of others, aided, as we are, by well equipped hot-houses and conditions most favorable. In trees they have dwarfed the most stately and beautiful into miniature form, some with long flowing leaves, others with waxen texture and

FIG. 39.—JAPANESE BANTAMS.

bright glowing colors. These are engrafted into one another until the product is a beautiful little toy tree with many kinds and colors of leaves. Even in the production of fruit trees they succeed in getting wonderful results.

A friend, who spent years of his life in their country, tells me that they take young fowls and animals and confine them in boxes made to suit their purpose, and of different forms to meet the form of their specimen. These are confined in the ill-shaped boxes until they mature and their bodies grow to the shape of the inside of the box. No consideration of time and trouble affects them just so they can accomplish the object in view and surpass a neighbor in the work. Think of a square shaped chicken or pig, or a squirrel or rabbit with a hump like a camel! These same efforts produced the fowls with the very long tails, many of which are little larger than our Bantams. To produce these curious freaks must take an extent of confinement on one hand and so close in-breeding on the other that they must possess some wonderful secret of infusing vigor into their specimens unknown to us.

Some thirty-five years ago the first fowls known as Japanese Bantams came to England. The early specimens were of cuckoo marking, others variously marked and speckled, but the most attractive were what we now call Black Tailed Japanese Bantams. No mention is made of the white edge on the sickle feathers of these early importations. We should presume from all information at hand that this was not prominent enough to cause any mention of same. In addition to the above mentioned varieties, some came frizzled feathered.

The Black Tailed Japanese are described as follows, by an early writer: "The cock has good carriage, short clear yellow legs, drooping wings with black flights, body white, tail erect with long black sickle feathers showing white shaft, comb large and upright, moderate serrations, wattles long and red. The hen should have a very short yellow leg, drooped wings, black flights, white body, tail large, erect and fan shaped, the hen's comb crinkled." Another description tells us there is another variety of White Japanese Bantams in which the cock's tail flows in a sweeping semi-circle. In perfect specimens the center of these feathers is of the deepest glossy black, finely edged or laced with white like the tail of a Silver Penciled Hamburg. The latter description was recorded about ten years after the first, showing that at this later date the edged tail was noticed. Today we have the preference for dark slate or black primaries, edged with white. The English standard calls for a black inner web for the wing primaries and secondaries. Both now call for white edge on tail in both sickle and coverts. The English also admit the following varieties at the present time: Black Tailed White, Black, White, Speckled, Buff, Gray, Brown and Cuckoo.

We present for consideration the description of a pair shown at the Palace Show, as described by an expert: "Cock, snowy white in feathers of neck, breast, thighs, body and wings, with a black tail; each sickle evenly edged with white; his legs and bill as yellow as an orange; comb, lobes and face as red as blood; when his wings are open they show the black in the underneath feathers of flights and coverts, but the upper and outer surfaces are white. The hen is colored just like the cock and her shape is like his." Why we should prefer the dark slate color for primary markings can hardly be told. Why should slate colored wing markings be preferred in these when it is not allowed in Light Brahmas, both being white with black markings? The comb of a Japanese is quite prominent and beautiful, usually fine in form and well serrated. The face, ear-lobes and wattles are quite uniform and handsome. A well formed Japanese female is a very quaint looking bird, the short legs, drooped wings and long tail being so very different from any other fowl, and when they move about they look almost as if they were sliding along.

No variety of fowls breeds more true than they, their main

fault being loss of color in the black feathers and defective lacing. To my notion the most attractive of all Japanese is the pure black. This color seems to fit their size and form better than the white with black tails. They are also to be had in solid white, buff, gray and brown of various shades. The most popular varieties are the Black Tailed Whites, pure Black and pure Whites.

The first importation of Black Tailed Whites into this country were quite oversized birds in comparison with those we now have. The first importation of real quality in Japanese Bantams, we believe, should be credited to Mr. J. D. Nevius, of Philadelphia, who has at different times had large consignments of Black Tailed Whites, pure Black, White and Grays of superior quality. The first really fine specimens seen by the writer were in his yards.

Black Tailed Whites are the best known with us. To breed them to perfection is quite an art. The proper coloring of body, wings and tail must be closely watched to prevent them fading or encroaching upon forbidden ground. The rich yellow color of beak, legs and toes; the bright red face, comb and wattles; pure white plumage of entire body; wings partly black; and black tails, the sickles and coverts of same edged with white, make a beautiful combination for the breeder's skill to work into greater perfection. Their long overbalancing tails and full plumage with their form and carriage of body give them an appearance unlike any other fowl. A slight description of their general form will represent them all as to shape.

The face of a Japanese Bantam should be full and round from a side view; eyes large and bright; comb rather large, strong and well serrated; neck short, curving backward over the body, almost touching the tail; back short; breast round and full with a forward carriage; body short and plump; wings long and drooping; the tail of the male long and full, carried upright and forward almost touching his head; the tail of the female should be carried nearly upright, a drooping or hanging to either side is quite a serious defect; legs very short and free from feathers, the shorter the shank the better, just so the body is carried free from the ground.

The Black Tailed variety should be a very clear white, all except wings and tail. The primaries should be black, edged with white. The secondaries, our standard tells us, should be dark slate, edged with white on the upper web, lower web white. We much prefer the black in wing of both male and female, tail of both black. In the male the sickles and coverts are edged all around with white. The tail coverts of female same as body color. If of fine form and carriage and pure white with black markings, this is a beautiful Bantam.

The Black Japanese Bantam should be a pure black, if of a greenish luster so much the more beautiful. Beaks, legs and toes in all Japanese Bantams should be yellow, but in Blacks they are apt to shade into a dark color. This is allowable, and is often seen on the richest colored specimens. The Whites should be pure white. The Grays, very dark or black in body color; the male marked in neck, back and wings much like a Silver Dorking; the female laced all over with the same silvery color. Such well marked specimens are very scarce.

FIG. 40.—FRIZZLED BANTAMS.

Usually the markings of both male and female are very deficient. A few Buff Japanese were shown at New York in 1897. They are very scarce and not fully developed as a distinct variety.

In breeding these Bantams the most perfect specimens obtainable should be bred together, not more than two or three females to each male. The young chicks must be very tenderly handled until six or eight weeks old. After reaching this age they are quite hardy and will care for themselves if properly fed and housed in dry quarters at night. Long grass makes a bad run for them when damp as they are quite sensitive to wet and damp surroundings. Being so close to the ground their body feathers get wet and produce disease.

FRIZZLED BANTAMS.

Frizzled Bantams of the Japanese type are quite like them in form. Some contend that they are of English origin, while others tell us they came from Japan. Their general appearance would indicate their close relationship. They look quite like the Japanese in shape and color. The plumage of the whole body turns a reversed way. We will treat more fully of them in our next chapter.

CHAPTER VIII.

FRIZZLED AND RUMPLESS BANTAMS.

Their Origin Must Be Oriental.

IN the chapter on Japanese fowls mention was made of the Frizzled as being of the same variety. In giving the information about these breeds, it is not my intention to claim all the statements as my own, for the reason that much of this information is gathered from books and recorded for your information. It is my wish to state here that the information thus gathered is put into this form without any reference to its origin.

The Frizzled is one of the oldest known breeds. Naturalists made mention of this and the Rumpless about three hundred years ago. On one point the early writers agree—that the Frizzled is a native of Southern Asia; also to be found in Java, Sumatra and the Phillippine Islands. The prevailing color of the wild race is white, with smooth legs. Some specimens were found of various colors and feathered legs, indicating the presence of the same blood that produced our Brahmas and Cochins. These facts would indicate an interchange of fowls at that early day between the inhabitants of the older nations of the earth. If the fowls of China found their way to the natives of the above named countries, why not the same interchange of fowls with Japan, thus giving them the blood to produce the Frizzled Japanese Bantams?

The Rumpless, called in early times the Rumpkin, is properly called "Choci-Kukullo," which translated is "Cochin Fowl." Some writers claim it as a native of Persia. Aldrovandus spoke of this variety as the Persian fowl, while others positively state that it first came from Cochin, and their natural color was black. Some white ones were also seen. These facts show that both these fowls originally came from the same region of the country, that their original color was black or white, with smooth legs, and for the Rumpless rose combs. The Frizzled were very much the same. Now, these facts being so plainly recorded at that early day should be a guide for our standard makers, and if recognized by them at all, color and comb should be very specific and positively described and held to, and not a lot of cross-bred mongrels encouraged into the show room.

Japan has sent us in the last twenty years many odd fowls, showing their ability to produce odd forms, the Frizzled one being the most attractive. Some of our ablest English writers do not admit that these came from Japan, but to my mind their form and carriage point to the Japanese origin. They are bred and shown in many colors, but the preference is given in all cases to Blacks and Whites, the former the most preferred. I copy from an English writer these words: "As to comb we have no great preference, though our choice would be the single comb, but in legs and feet, four toes and clean legs are to be preferred. Of all the Frizzled, Whites seem to be the most charming. These should have yellow legs (often they are willow, sometimes slate), but yellow should have the preference. Next come the Golden, with yellow or willow legs; the Slate color, with black or slate colored legs, and the Blacks with black legs. In addition to these, we have the Browns, Grays and Blues,—in fact, all kinds of solid and mixed colors known to fowls." These statements show the many different colors of these little frizzled fowls.

Frizzled Bantams are quite small, some of the Palace winners not exceeding one pound in weight. The most valued property is the curl of the feathers, next, the quality of feather; to be perfect they must be hard and wiry. Color is the third consideration. Being a tender fowl they must be protected from all changes of the weather, rain or storms. They are fairly good layers, splendid sitters and mothers, and their chicks are as easily raised as the Japanese.

The Rumpless Bantams, produced, as they were, by Mr. Tegetmeier, seem to my mind to belong to the same chapter with the above. Let me quote the words of others as to them: "They were produced by a cross of a very small Rumpless hen with a crest. She was mated to a White Polish and produced Rumpless Polish Bantams. This same hen mated to a very small Nankin Bantam produced tailless Nankins. The result of these two crosses passed into the hands of others, who continued the work and produced them in many forms and colors; also some with very short, booted legs. Both single and rose combs are seen, but the single is much preferred." These two breeds in their many colors would make a study for any number of fanciers, and I hope some enterprising breeder will look into them and add them in perfection to our list of little beauties at our exhibitions.

CHAPTER IX.

NANKIN BANTAMS.

One of the Most Ancient Breeds of Bantams, originally Called Nankeen.

THESE little beauties came into notice many, many years ago, and they have taken part in the make-up of more of their kind than any one bird. They are seldom seen in England, and we hardly think a single specimen is owned in America at this time. For their description, I must depend on the writings of others. Comb may be single or double, the best of early days had single combs; legs blue. Some had white legs, but my opinion is that the double combs and white legs came from a cross with other birds. When bred in England color of legs and style of comb did not matter so all in one pen were alike. Thus the two competed. These birds were quite neglected until they fell into the hands of game keepers, who use them for rearing partridges. Mr. Cresswell brought them into notice early in the seventies, by exhibiting a beautiful pen at the Crystal Palace Show. He preferred the double combs and white legs. I give our readers his description of them: "Size as small as possible, comb single or double, the latter preferred; legs blue or white, the former are preferred, but hard to find; the birds of my original stock had white legs. As long as these birds match in show pens the comb and color of legs are not essential points."

The cock has an amusing and conceited walk, with flowing sickle, tail and wings almost sweeping the ground. His breast and body are of a deep ginger color; the back, wings, coverts, neck and saddle a rich, orange chestnut; tail, dark chestnut, shading into black, almost like the original Cochin Bantams in color. The hen's general color is a clear buff; like a Buff Cochin. Dark, medium and light colored birds are found among them. Most of them have a shaded or penciled hackle, but they should be free from this, with tails brown, shading into black at the ends. The unseen half of primary in both male and female is often black. They are naturally very domestic and tame, excellent layers of good sized eggs and careful mothers for their chicks. They breed very true to form and color. The fact that these birds breed so true to their own type proves their originality. If taken in hand by experts of the present day they would soon become a favorite, both for their beauty and sterling qualities. Since writing the above, Mr. John Glasgow has secured and bred some of these little beauties of most perfect form and feather.

CUCKOO BANTAMS.

Cuckoo Bantams, or miniature Scotch Greys, are like our American Dominiques. They have single combs and white legs. They are produced both in Scotland and England quite independently. Another variety of these same birds has been produced by crossing them with Rose Combs, giving them the rose combs and darker legs. These crosses produce Cuckoo color with rose combs, Andalusian color and light slate blue color, also both white and black with both styles of combs. These Bantams are almost lost sight of, having been pushed aside by the many new kinds more handsome of form and feather.

In my boyhood days we had the African Bantam, or Crow chicken, very small and finely built. In form they were very much like the early Games, the male being marked very much like our present Brown Leghorns and the females perfectly black. These little fowls bred as true as sparrows year after year. I bred from the product of the one original pair. They had for their home a big box covered with stiff paper and painted with tar, the roof made of boards to shed the water. Here winter and summer they grew and thrived under conditions that our present fowls could not stand. They had all the corn they could eat, but their size kept just the same. These fowls came by steamer to Philadelphia to a man who had a paper mill. He bred from them and sent their product to the children of his sister, and from them came my pair from which I bred for years with no new blood. This experience illustrates the constitutional powers of these small fowls. Follow this plan with judgment, and form, size and color are at your command in handling and reducing these small fowls.

CHAPTER X.

POLISH BANTAMS.

Also Some New Bantams Worthy of Note.

THESE miniature Polish are of the same form, colors and marking as their larger relatives of the same name. Both American and English fanciers have worked to produce these little beauties. The lack of general interest in them proves a barrier to their progress, and it may be their extermination. They are a most beautiful little fowl, and a Polish Bantam craze that would result in a club that would push these little beauties to the front might soon result in a special Polish Bantam show that would rival the New York cat show or the Boston exclusive pigeon show.

These Bantams have been bred in the following colors: Black, white, buff, silver, gold, cuckoo, blue, and white crested black. They are simply Polish Bantams with all the Polish markings, etc., that belong to the Polish family. They were produced by crossing Golden Polish and Golden Sebright Bantams for the golden color. For the silver color, Silver Polish and Silver Sebrights were used. For Black and White Polish, Black and White Rose Comb Bantams were used. These crosses produced solid Blacks and Whites, and White Crested Blacks; also white crested blue or slate colored and solid colored blues. The pure Whites were among the first to attract attention both here and in England. Up to the present time they are the most perfect of all Polish Bantams. Of them we shall make particular mention.

White Crested White Polish Bantams only are allowed by our standard; no other Polish Bantam is considered. Of these, two kinds or forms of comb are allowed—the single and V-shaped. Birds of the single comb variety have silvery white colored legs and no beard, while those that have the V-shaped combs have blue or slate colored legs, and a beard or muff under the throat, extending back to crest on either side. The beak of each conforms in color with the legs, either silver or blue, as may be. The blue colored legs, V-shaped combs, and beards, we believe were produced both in this country and England at about the same time. The others may show signs of an unnatural cross. Demanding, as we do, V or leaf combs and blue legs for standard White Polish, why should we admit both in the Bantams? Then, as to weight, there is only two ounces difference in these Polish Bantams and a Buff Cochin Bantam. These points show a very unnatural standard's demands. The English demand seventeen to twenty-two ounces for males and fourteen to eighteen ounces for females in all Polish Bantams. Why should our standard permit such heavy weights for them?

The White Polish Bantams should be pure white and as small as possible. Our preference is for the V or leaf comb. Having, as they do, the muff or beard, and being naturally the better formed Bantam, they should have the preference. To breed these successfully, select a male perfect in form, crest and beard; he should also have a large, well-proportioned tail for his size. Legs should be of blue color and very smooth. His beak should also be blue and crest should be large and perfect in form. He should be mated to a small female as perfect in all these points as possible. A hen should be preferred rather than a pullet for producing strong chicks. It is always best to select as breeding stock birds that have the largest knobs for the crest to grow upon. Always select a crest that is well filled in front and as round as possible.

The other variety is or should be the same, only the single comb as small as possible. They have silver colored legs and beaks, in other points the same, only no beard.

In all other varieties of Polish Bantams the standard for the larger varieties should guide, excepting the size. This in all Polish Bantams should be quite small. Do not try to produce these beautiful fowls and call them Bantams when half the size of the larger Polish. Their beauty depends on their miniature size.

Since writing the above Mr. F. B. Zimmer, of Gloversville, N. Y., has shown me his flock of Bearded White Crested White Polish, and produced evidence to show me that he was not only the first to produce this variety, but the only one thus far to produce them of proper size and shape with all the other features of this variety in so marked a degree as to assure reproduction of their high qualities. His strain of Bearded White Polish is, beyond all dispute, the best in all the world.

A new variety of Polish Bantams is just now before us—the Buff Laced Polish Bantams. To be of correct type they must resemble the larger Polish of the same variety in all features and conform in size to other Polish Bantams.

THE SULTAN OR BOOTED WHITE POLISH.

The Sultan or Booted White Polish we mentioned with the Booted Bantams. Nothing could be more beautiful than nice, well-kept Sultans. They would help to swell the numbers for a Polish Bantam club.

SILKY BANTAMS.

The Silky Bantams are very scarce, and are known of the following varieties: Whites, Yellow or Golden, Browns or Blacks. Some of these have single combs, others the walnut comb. They are quite small, rather hairy, and said to be good sitters and mothers. Their native land was Eastern Asia, about Malacca. Early writers call them the woolly hen. Their feathers being almost entirely fluff give them the woolly appearance. Their skin and bones are of a purple or blue color. This makes a distasteful looking dish for the table, for when cooked they have a dark uninviting appearance. In the early days of the Cochin some of them were called Silky Cochins, their plumage being fluffy to the very end of the feathers, showing the influence of home cultivation of the fancy in the Orient. Thus writes an early fancier of these fowls: "Silkies may be classed as purely fancy, having only their own peculiarities to recommend them. In place of feathers they have silky hair; the skin and legs are blue; face and comb deep purple; ear lobes tinged with white. The best of them have five toes and pure white plumage."

A BREEDER OF POLISH.

GLOVERSVILLE, N. Y., March 13, 1897.
Mr. T. F. McGrew:

Sixteen to seventeen years ago I started in the plain Polish Bantams, and thirteen or fourteen years ago I brought out the entire original stock. They originated in Massachusetts, near Agawam, as much by accident as any way. At about that time (thirteen or fourteen years) there was as good as none outside of my flock. The standard just let them in and, as you know, called for single comb and white legs. (I do not know who made this standard.) Many of the chicks had blue legs and I was not as particular then as I am now and sold lots of these disqualified birds after telling customers, but they were crazy after them, so they went. Being interested personally, I have kept my eyes open for Polish Bantams, and I never saw an English bird that was white, nor heard of one, with V comb and blue legs in America. And after I wrote our bearded standard as it now reads, I never heard of any English being imported and am certain all those that are being shown in America now are from my stock, that I bred from Big Bearded English Polish and my non-bearded birds. I will not assert that England never had a bird to conform to our standard of Bearded Bantams.

F. B. ZIMMER.

THE BANTAM FOWL

NEW BANTAMS

The desire to produce new breeds is almost a craze with us. Not content with improving those we have, our attention

FIG. 41.—GOLD DUST CHAMPION—BUFF COCHIN BANTAM.
Bred by T. F. McGrew.

is attracted toward new things. The new rule adopted by the American Poultry Association will close the door, for some time at least, against imitation breeds or varieties, as may be.

As a matter of record, I will mention a number of styles and kinds of Bantams that have come and gone, many of them with merely passing notice. The most attractive of these are the Penciled and Spangled Hamburg Bantams. They can be produced by crossing Hamburgs and Sebrights together, and reduced by inbreeding and selection. The Silver Penciled of these varieties is the most attractive, and we have seen some fairly good ones for the first cross.

Minorca, Andalusian, and Leghorn Bantams of fairly good form can be produced by proper crosses and inbreeding. We have seen Andalusian Bantams of fairly good color and comb, fashioned after the old style of Game Bantams. Brown Leghorn Bantams can be produced by crossing a small Brown Leghorn male with an old style Black Red Game Bantam hen. Inbreed and select the most perfect specimens of small size and breed from them late chicks. White Leghorns can be produced in the same manner using small White Games for the cross.

Bantams called Centurions, buff in color, resembling White Wonders, are bred by crossing Golden Sebrights, Japanese and Buff Cochin Bantams with Buff Wyandottes. In our opinion the same or better results might be obtained by crossing the Golden Sebright on the Buff Cochin Bantam. This would give the buff color, the feathered legs and rose comb in much shorter time than the other numerous crosses. Buff Plymouth Rock and Buff Wyandotte Bantams are produced by similar crosses. In fact, almost every known fowl has to-day its counterpart in miniature form of more or less merit. This may do very well as a pastime, to please the fancy of those who produce them, but to have any real value they must possess the characteristics of the breed they imitate and reproduce of their kind moderately perfect specimens.

BURMESE BANTAMS

This variety of Bantams came to Scotland from Bermah about fifteen years ago. They are a small white Bantam when in their best form, but black, brown and speckled colors are also natural to the breed. They have a crest on their heads, single small comb in front of the crest, long wings, very long tails, extremely short legs, in fact so short that their breast and body almost touches the ground. Their short, heavily feathered legs and toes make it difficult for them to move about. The legs and beaks of the Burmese are yellow, and from their general description we should think they were much like the Japanese, with heavy leg and toe featherling and crest added.

BLACK SPANISH BANTAMS

Our attention has been called to the fact that they now have in England a most perfect little Black Spanish Bantam, about the size of the Rose Comb Bantam. It is claimed that they are perfect little beauties, with all the features well developed.

Houdan Bantams, Dorking Bantams and Creve Coeur Bantams have made their appearance in England, in a small way, in the last ten years. All of them are splendid models of the larger fowls they miniature. None of these have as yet made any prominence for themselves. So far they are only a matter of record. The most prominent new variety of Bantams is the Langshan now being pushed for honors by their originator, Mr. Hughes, whose description of them is given below:

BLACK LANGSHAN BANTAMS

In general appearance they are just like the Black Langshans; in fact, a perfect counterpart of them in miniature form. They also have their egg producing trait. They were produced by breeding in direct line from Black Langshans by proper selecting and mating and now breed true to size and form; in fact, they breed so true that a large per cent of them are quite good enough for either exhibition or breeding.

Now a few words regarding how I came to breed them. In the fall of 1892 a Black Langshan hen stole her nest and hatched a brood of chicks in November. The flock which had this hen as a member was running at large in an old orchard and I did not see either the hen or chicks until snow came and I looked to see if all the stock was roosting in the house; then I found the chicks. Well, my first thought on seeing them

FIG. 42.—WHITE COCHIN BANTAM.
Snow Drop, from life. Bred at Elmwood Farm.

was, "How much they look like Bantams!" These chicks, five of them, survived the winter, and the thought that they looked like Bantams was father to the resolve to try and breed from them Black Langshan Bantams. The chicks were dwarfed in size and to-day two of the hens that were the foundation of the O. K. strain of Black Langshan Bantams are alive and only weigh three pounds each.

As to how I succeeded in my resolve to breed and establish a strain of Black Langshan Bantams I refer the reader and others interested to my past exhibits of them.

WILLIAM M. HUGHES.

CHAPTER XI.

PREPARING FOR EXHIBITION.

THE proper time to begin preparing a bird for exhibition is when selecting the parent bird for the breeding pen. Perfect health and condition are quite as necessary in the parent bird as in the offspring; the former will not produce healthy stock if in poor condition, unhealthy birds will not make exhibition birds of true value, for such birds will not stand the preparation necessary to condition them for competition, and without such condition the chances of winning are very poor.

After twenty-five years of experience in poultry exhibitions all over the country, I am fully prepared to say that the successful exhibitor of fancy fowls is always either an expert at conditioning birds or a successful purchaser from those who understand the art. Never in all my experience have I seen a poorly conditioned bird win in strong competition. When this is considered in its true light we fully appreciate the necessity of having exhibition stock in the highest show condition. This includes perfect health, perfect plumage, high condition of flesh (not overly fat) and perfect cleanliness from tip of comb to end of toes. Not one single section can be overlooked or neglected in its preparation, if success is to be assured.

To properly rear a bird for exhibition it must be well looked after from the day it is hatched. It will not answer to allow them to grow up as they may and then select the best for exhibition; they must be properly fed, watered, housed, and kept clean and free from all insects and diseases. In Bantams they must be fed quite enough to keep them growing properly, but not overfed so as to force them to oversize. Good health and condition must be maintained. And, above all, never allow your birds to run about in the wet after cool weather begins in the fall. If perfectly dry the cold will not injure them.

When fully matured, handle Bantams in preparation for exhibition as follows: All smooth legged varieties should be kept busy hunting in hay or straw for all they get to eat. The litter must be clean and dry. This continued digging gives a fine polish to feet, legs and plumage of the birds; hardens their flesh and keeps them under standard weight. The feather legged birds must be continually watched to prevent their scratching and destroying the feathers on their feet. Small coops must be provided for them, the floors of the same covered with clean, dry pine sawdust. All food should be given in dishes; great care should be taken not to drop any of the food on the floor of the coop, for this will induce them to scratch and break the foot feathering. The sawdust must be put through a coarse sieve each day to free it from all dirt and droppings, for thus only can perfect cleanliness be observed.

All smooth legged, close feathered varieties should have their plumage polished at least once a day with a cotton flannel cloth or a silk handkerchief. This will keep them perfectly clean and free from any bad condition of plumage, and add luster and finish to same. Never use oil of any kind upon the feathers, for while it looks well for a few days, it soon gathers dust and dirt, thus destroying the rich appearance of surface plumage.

By keeping the legs of your fowls perfectly clean and nicely polished with a woolen cloth or chamois skin, no roughness or bad color will appear; when neglected it takes so much hard rubbing to make them presentable, that they often have the appearance of having been scaled to the quick. When this is carried to excess and the spurs shelled it gives the legs the appearance of raw meat. This should count against the specimen in the show pen.

The proper training for the show pen is of great importance. No good excuse can be offered for placing a wild, untrained specimen in the show room. It is quite impossible to properly consider the good or bad points of such applicants for honors; but few of them can be considered as a factor in a closely contested class. All birds intended for show purposes should be trained to stand in the most attractive positions, and be taught to allow any one at all times and in all places to handle them and remove them from their coops. When thus taught to put their best front forward, if of good quality and condition, all is done that can be done. Such a specimen has considerable in its favor as against one that has no training for the show pen.

WASHING FOR EXHIBITION.

Almost every one who has found it necessary to wash his fowls for exhibition follows methods and ways of his own. Some use hot suds and a sponge; others, alcohol to clean the spots from the plumage, and others brush the outside or surface plumage with hot suds and a stiff brush. All these methods are good, if they succeed.

My plan is as follows: Fill a tub, (or bucket of the proper size to meet the demands for room according to the size of the bird to be washed), with warm water. First wash head, comb, face and wattles with a small hand brush; use a very little soap for same. Next scrub feet and legs very clean with same brush. If the fowl has feathers on legs and feet, wash quite clean with plenty of soap. When these parts are perfectly clean put the whole body of the fowl into the water and thoroughly soften the feathers. As soon as the feathers are well soaked with the water rub them through and through with plenty of soap; use your hands and fingers for this. Work the soap well into the skin; wash them as if you wished to get every spot of dirt off the skin. When satisfied that the under plumage and skin has been well cleaned by thoroughly washing every spot with your fingers, then wash the surface plumage with your hands and plenty of soap. When satisfied that all has been well washed dip the whole bird under water and with your hands wash the feathers thoroughly and free them as much as possible from the soap. Then thoroughly rinse in a tub or bucket of clean, warm water. When the feathers are perfectly free from all soap and dirt, then plunge the whole bird into clean, cold water. When removed from this dry the feathers as much as possible with cloths or towels. Always rub the proper way of the feathers. When as much water as possible is worked from the feathers in this way, take the fowl by the legs, allow its head to hang down and swing gently so the wings will flap and plumage be loosened.

The most important part of the operation is the proper drying of the plumage. The best way to dry the plumage is to place the bird in a very hot room; a room that is heated with steam is the best. If the hot room is not convenient place the bird in a coop close to a warm stove or open fire. Great care must be used not to allow the face or comb to blister before the hot fire. To properly dry the plumage the fowl must be kept in a very warm place till perfectly dry. The feathers must be all quite dry through and through, or they will stick together and look very bad. If dried quickly in a very warm room the feathers will web out nicely and look beautiful and fresh. If poorly done they will look worse than before. It is better to make the first attempt at washing a fowl with one of little value. Do not experiment with one of your best fowls. Learn the lesson first and then work with the exhibition stock. Always put some blue in the rinse water for white fowls, about as you would for white clothes.

When preparing birds for exhibition remember that fine condition goes far towards their winning, and nothing helps more than perfectly clean plumage, legs and feet; so in preparing them use great care in washing any part that may need cleansing, or, if necessary, the whole bird.

CHAPTER XII.

DISEASES OF BANTAMS.

How to Prevent and Cure Them.

BANTAMS when young have many dangers confronting them. Being so small, of necessity they are tender and delicate. Sudden changes of the weather during the night will often cause them to droop and look out of good condition, but with care they will prosper as well as their larger relations. To prevent disease be positively certain that the parent birds have no taint of any kind about them. Positive absence of all disease in the breeding stock is first to be considered. When the eggs are set under the hen, she and the nest must both be perfectly free from dirt or lice, and the hen must be in perfect health. To make doubly sure, dust the hen well with insect powder (Persian is the best) before placing her on the eggs, and again one week before due to hatch. This should destroy all insect life; but do not trust it. In addition give the hen a good dust bath for her use during incubating; and when the chicks are hatched look sharp for their first enemy, the head louse, usually to be found, if present, on top of the head. They may locate on the neck. If none are present you may conclude the chick is safe for a week from them. When any are found, paint well the head and neck with melted lard, a little warm—not hot. Use small, stiff, flat brush, and be sure the head and neck are oiled well to the skin. This will destroy all that may be present; but keep a close watch against their return.

More young Bantams die from diarrhea than from all other causes. People usually concede that the food they eat is the cause of the disease; they change the diet, and then wonder what makes the trouble. Nine times out of ten it is caused by taking cold in some way; bad or sour food will cause it; want of grit or too much water after a long thirst will produce the same result. The best remedy is to give them special care so that none of the above causes will exist. Should the chicks be so affected, clear all obstruction from the vent by removing the soiled down with a pair of scissors, using great care not to cut the skin. Anoint with fresh olive oil and feed dry cooked food. Always provide plenty of good, sharp sand, or very small grit for them. I feed nothing but Spratt's Bantam Food and bread crumbs until they are over three weeks old.

The next trouble for the little Bantam is cold. Until fully feathered they are very susceptible to changes in the weather. Cold, damp days and nights often work havoc among them. The only sure preventive for this is to house them in a well-constructed coop, having a covered run, where they can enjoy partial freedom during bad weather. When affected feed warm, rich food, keep them dry, and tie a lump of camphor and a small stone in a piece of white muslin and drop this into their drinking water. The stone is for a sinker; camphor is good for cold in all cases. If Bantams are kept free from lice, cold and dampness, and properly fed and watered, they will be free from every disease.

ROUP.

This name is applied to all stages of the ailment, from a slight cold to the most disgusting diphtheritic condition. Sometime since a statement appeared in one of our journals, saying that young chicks never have the roup. The author has discovered that the above is incorrect. Being asked to look at a brood of chicks that were hatched where no other chickens had been for several years, he found them to be about three weeks old and affected with roup and canker of the very worst kind—eyes swollen and an offensive discharge from the nostrils. This proves that it can come at any time. No doubt such cases start from diseased parent birds.

How to cure roup is a question hard to settle. If in the stage of a slight cold, clean the mouth, throat, nostrils and head with warm water and soap, rinse well with warm water and vinegar, half of each. Take a small syringe and force some of this warm mixture through both nostrils till well cleaned. Follow this with an injection of olive oil. Place the bird in warm, dry quarters and feed soft food. If this does not improve the patient and it grows worse you will save time by destroying the specimen and burning the carcass.

Another treatment is to cleanse them as above and give Aconite or Arsenicum. Others say Spongia in their drinking water is a good remedy. All these methods will help some of those afflicted with the disease; but when the case is so bad that they grow worse each day under such care, it is better to kill them.

I have seen specimens cured by dipping the head in a can of oil (kerosene.) This will also remove all the feathers from the head, but they come again. So many call a simple cold the roup. Usually when cured by any reasonable means it is a simple cold, but real roup in a fowl is as bad as diphtheria in a child and as hard to cure.

The following on disease is printed by permission of Dr. Wm. Y. Fox, of Taunton, Mass.:

COLD.

A common cold is probably the most prevalent disease the human family is subject to, and the same is true of Bantams. The first symptom is sneezing, then a discharge of clear, watery fluid from the nostrils and eyes; later, a slight loss of appetite and general dumpishness.

In itself a cold is of little consequence, but, as it is often the forerunner of roup, it must not be neglected. Cold is generally caused by drafts blowing across the roosts at night, or by filthy quarters. It may also be caused by dampness in the house or runs, or too much exposure to bad weather. Bantams can be allowed in their yards in very cold weather if the ground is free from snow and mud, but they are much better off in the house if there is mud or snow on the ground, or if it is stormy. In this respect they certainly require more care than the large varieties. The prevention of colds lies in keeping the flock in clean, tight, dry quarters.

The treatment is very simple. If only one or two are affected remove them from the rest and place in a coop where they will be warm and free from drafts. Get some camphorated oil, at any drug store, and with a small glass syringe inject it into the nostrils twice a day. This will generally effect a cure within a few days. If many of the flock are afflicted in this way it will be impracticable to treat separately, and the first thing to do is to find and remove the cause of the illness. Having done this, keep a small piece of gum camphor in the drinking water and watch carefully for further symptoms. Do not allow the nostrils to become plugged by a crust, as they often will, because the discharge will be held back and act as poison.

After the nostrils have been obstructed a day or two the head will begin to swell and before we know it we have a case of roup to deal with. The injection of camphorated oil as already directed will usually keep the nostrils free and open.

ROUP.

This is a contagious disease, and generally begins as a simple cold. It is often fatal, and is much to be dreaded as it will sometimes go through the whole flock before the owner is aware that there is any serious trouble. It is difficult to say just when a cold turns into roup, but when the discharge from the nostrils and eyes becomes thick and sticky, and of an offensive odor, you may be sure that you have a case of roup. The next symptom is swelling of the head and eyes; frequently the eyelids will stick together, and if washed apart a large amount of fetid matter will escape. As these symptoms increase the bird is growing sicker all the time, more dumpish and has little or no appetite.

Roup may be prevented by good care and prompt treatment of every cold, but above all by care in introducing new birds into the flock. Whenever you buy a new hen keep her in quarantine at least two weeks, until you are sure she is in perfect health, before exposing your stock to the danger of contagion. Bantams of a strong, vigorous constitution, properly housed and fed, will never have roup, unless they catch it from some diseased fowl carelessly introduced into their house.

Probably the most common way for the disease to be transmitted from one to another, is through the drinking water. Be careful to thoroughly clean and scald any drinking vessel that has been used by any sick Bantam, before using it again. It is doubtful whether the disease can be carried in the air, but give the well birds the benefit of the doubt and confine diseased ones in separate houses or rooms. It is unwise to keep an invalid in a room with a fire, unless you are prepared to keep him there until warm weather, for it will never be safe to return the convalescent patient to the unheated house after he has had the luxury of a fire.

The treatment of roup is, in the main, very unsatisfactory, although, if begun soon enough it may save a valuable specimen. Keep the nostrils, eyes and throat as clean as possible. Get a bottle of listerine at any drug store, and put a tablespoonful into a glass of warm water. Inject into the nostrils, swab the throat and wash the head and eyes with it two or three times a day for the first four or five days. Feed with soft cooked food and milk.

If this treatment makes no improvement in the patient, kill him and burn his carcass. This is the kindest and best advice that can be given, for, although he may recover after weeks of dosing and pampering, he will still be a weak bird and the slightest exposure will start a discharge from the nostrils, which may contain the germs of roup and be sufficient to cause the disease in the flock to which he belongs.

A Bantam that has once had a genuine severe attack of roup is never fit to breed from, as his offspring will be sickly, puny chicks nine times out of ten. If you are unwilling to take this advice, as you probably will be until you have tried to cure roup yourself, the next best thing to do is to continue to keep head and nostrils as clean as possible. Stop the aconite and give one grain of sulphate of quinine three times a day, and all the milk and whisky you can pour down, every three or four hours. By this time your pet will not eat and his strength must be kept up by forcing the whisky and milk. Should your efforts prove successful and the bird begins to mend, leave off the whisky and quinine very gradually and put enough tincture of chloride of iron into the drinking water to give a decided brown color; feed good cooked food and a little meat once a day.

CANKER OR DIPHTHERITIC ROUP.

This is a frequent accompaniment of ordinary roup, and is probably a different manifestation of the same disease. It is highly contagious to other fowl and possibly to man. Cases are reported where children have probably contracted diphtheria from fowls sick with canker, and also where poultry that have had access to discharges from diphtheria patients have sickness with canker. The one distinguishing symptom of canker is the appearance in the mouth or throat of a white or yellowish white cheesy membrane. This may appear during the course of ordinary roup, or may come on suddenly in an apparently healthy fowl. At the first onset one or more white spots, about the size of a pin head, may be seen either on the roof of the mouth or under the tongue, or, quite often around the opening to the wind pipe. These spots grow very rapidly until, often times, the whole mouth is filled with a membrane that is usually glistening white, sometimes yellowish. When torn off it leaves a bleeding surface beneath. It is of very offensive odor. If this membrane extends into the wind pipe the patient will soon die of suffocation. This is a disease that can not be mistaken, as the appearance of the membrane is very characteristic.

The remarks on the cause and prevention of roup apply especially to canker and need not be repeated. The general treatment is also the same, but the local treatment is different. Instead of washing out nostrils and mouth attempts must be made to remove the membrane. This is often done by scraping with a piece of pine wood whittled to a convenient shape. After removing all that can be removed, without excessive bleeding, the parts should be powdered over with alum. A better way is to apply peroxide of hydrogen in full strength directly to the membrane, which will soon be eaten away with much less bleeding than in the other proceeding. After using the peroxide a few minutes, apply tincture of the chloride of iron in full strength. The mouth can be pretty well cleaned by either method, but the membrane soon returns and the process must be repeated often. When the membrane is in the wind pipe it has to be left to nature, and almost always proves fatal.

CHOLERA.

At the present day this is an extremely rare disease in the United States. It is the most contagious of the diseases of poultry, generally killing the whole flock when it once gets a foothold. It is always caused by contact with a previous case, never originating in a yard without such contact or exposure.

The symptoms are excessive diarrhea, first of a black substance as thick as tar, later by a thin, watery fluid which smells putrid. There is very rapid emaciation and prostration, death frequently occurring within thirty-six hours after the commencement of the disease. There is no treatment; kill and cremate.

DIARRHEA

This is quite frequent, and is sometimes mistaken for cholera, but cholera is so very rapid that this mistake ought not to be made. Diarrhea is usually caused by improper food, impure water, by sudden changes in temperature or exposure to cold and wet. Individual mild cases require no treatment, as they will soon recover. In severe cases, remove the patient to a coop, keep without food for twenty-four hours, keep lime water before it instead of clear water. After twenty-four hours give a little bread, soaked in boiled milk. Let this be the only food until diarrhea ceases. When there are a number of cases in the flock, be sure there is something wrong in food or drink. Search carefully for this cause and remove it.

CROP BOUND.

This is quite common in Bantams, and if not properly treated is very apt to prove fatal. The first symptom is a constant effort to swallow. The neck is stretched out, the mouth opened, and the hen acts the way you often see a little chick act when trying to get down a worm one size larger than his gullet.

The patient acts dumpish and stands in a peculiar position with the breast bone pitched forward and down. He is hungry and will keep eating until his crop is filled full and as hard as a stone. If you suspect that you have a case of crop bound place the subject where he can not eat for twenty-four hours and then feel his crop; if it is hard, or harder than when he was shut up, your suspicions are confirmed.

This trouble is caused by a plugging up of the outlet of the crop with some particle of food, such as a long, ribbon-like piece of hay or grass. It may be caused by overeating, as when fowls get access to the grain bin and then drink a lot of water. The cause in this case is, probably, not so much obstruction of the outlet as it is a paralysis of the muscles of the crop from overdistension. This is rather an unusual form of crop bound and is merely mentioned to point this moral; when you know your Bantams have enormously overeaten, deprive them of water until their crops are, at least, half empty. There is no way to prevent the other or obstructive form.

The treatment is the same in either case; empty the crop. This can sometimes be done by pouring castor oil down the throat and working the mass in the crop around with the fingers. Try this about three times, two or three hours apart. If by that time the mass is not softened it is time to resort to surgery. Remove the feathers from a space the size of a silver dollar directly over the crop. With a clean, sharp knife make a cut one and one-half inches long through the skin; pull the wound along about half an inch and with a second cut go directly through into the crop. With a spoon handle scoop out the contents thoroughly. Either see or feel the outlet of the crop, so as to remove any obstruction there may be there. Wash the inside of the crop and the wound with warm water, to which a little salt has been added. With a needleful of white silk sew up the crop and then the skin.

Give no food or drink for thirty-six hours, then give a little bread soaked in milk. Feed carefully for a week; by that time the little fellow will be all right, that is, supposing the relief to have been given soon enough. For, if the mass in the crop has fermented badly, as it will in three or four days, it will have excited so much inflammation that the operation does no good. Do not delay in a case of crop bound as twenty-four hours frequently make the difference between saving and losing a valuable bird.

LEG WEAKNESS.

This is most common in growing chickens and is shown by inability to stand up. The chicken appears hungry, and all right in every way, except that it tries to get around on its hock joints instead of its feet. This occurs either while the first feathers or the second are growing. It is due to defective nutrition and is analogous to what we frequently term in children as growing too fast for their strength. The remedy is to change the diet, giving more meat and cut bone, something to make more muscle. Take care that the other chicks do not prevent the weak one from getting any food at all. With a little care these cases recover in a few days.

In the full grown Bantam a similar condition is often seen, although not so often as in the heavy breeds, and is more apt to be due to rheumatism or cramp, the result of dampness or exposure. The remedy in these cases is to place the patient in a dry coop and feed well, at the same time rubbing the legs well with any good liniment.

SCALY LEGS.

This is a most disgusting affection and its presence in a flock is a sure sign of laziness or indifference on the part of the owner. It is caused by a parasite, and is, therefore, a contagious disease. When it first appears the shanks and toes become covered with a dry scaly substance which increases quite fast until it forms crusts so thick as to obscure entirely the original shape and color of the legs. It is most common among the feathered legged varieties, and spreads much faster in damp, filthy quarters than in clean, dry ones.

The treatment is very simple, but is also very effective. Apply thoroughly, with the fingers, some carbolized vaseline to every part of the shanks and toes. Repeat every two days until the legs are clean. Each time it is found that considerable scale may be rubbed off with the fingers, and it is advisable to remove all that will come off without causing bleeding In mild cases three applications is enough to effect a cure. In severe ones it may take six or seven, and, in such cases, it is well to repeat twice a month for three or four months after the case is apparently cured, as it otherwise is very liable to return.

LICE.

If you have had no experience with poultry you will probably smile when you see lice classed among the diseases, but after one or two broods have succumbed to their ravages, and the grown fowls all look as if they were in the last stages of consumption, you will admit that the little vermin are worthy of the first place in the list of diseases.

There are several varieties of lice which infest the hen house. There is the common white or gray louse, which is the largest and stick to the fowl day and night. The same variety is found on young chicks and is commonly called the head louse because oftenest found on the head and fastened to the skin like a leach. Then there is the red louse, or red mite, which works only at night. During the day he will be found under or on the roosting pole, or on the sides of the house. He is bright red, round and rather smaller than the head of a pin. Frequently these mites will congregate on a part of the wall so thick that one would think the wall was covered with fresh blood.

There is also a brown louse, larger than the red and not so large as the white. The habits of this are similar to both the others, that is to say, many will leave the fowl in the day time and be found in the house, but some of the more greedy will keep at work day and night. This is the kind that bothers the sitting hen the most. Sometimes she is compelled to leave her eggs, and, in such instances, one looking into the nest will see no eggs there, as they will be completely covered with a mass of the dirty brown lice.

The symptoms produced by lice are unmistakable, where one has once become acquainted with them. In a fowl there is ruffled plumage, white comb, great uneasiness and emaciation. In chicks there is weakness and drooping, sometimes diarrhea and a peculiar, characteristic look about the head, as if the beak had been pulled on and the head elongated. The proof that the symptoms are caused by lice is to see the enemy.

In this connection a very good answer appeared in the notes and queries of a recent poultry paper. The question was like this: "What is the matter with my chickens, they have such and such symptoms?" Answer, "Look for lice, and if you find them remove by doing thus and so. If you do not find any do just the same, for they are there, only you do not know how to look for them."

In looking for lice on fowl, look close to the skin around the vent and under wings; on chicks, examine head and under wings; in the house, look on under side of roost and into all the cracks and crevices.

The prevention and treatment are identical. Keep dropping-board clean in hot weather; sprinkle slaked lime over it occasionally. Have the roosts and dropping-board arranged so that they can easily be removed. Take them out in the yard twice a month, in summer, and paint them all over with kerosene, at the same time paint walls and cracks near where roosts belong. That same night go into the house and sprinkle a little Lambert's Death to Lice over the back of each hen. Clean out the nest boxes and paint inside and out with kerosene. Refill with clean nesting material and sprinkle a little Lambert's Death to Lice in it. Never set a hen without dusting both her and the nest thoroughly with the same powder, and repeat at least three times while she is sitting. When the chicks hatch, welcome them with a good dose of Lambert's, and repeat, at least once a week, for the first two months of their lives. There are probably other insecticides as good as Lambert's Death to Lice, but I have never seen them, and as I know that that will do the work, I do not hesitate to recommend it.

If the chicks are badly infested with head lice, the quickest way to relieve them is to apply a very little vaseline to the top of their heads and under their wings. After one application of this the free use of Death to Lice will keep them away. Do not forget to keep the chicken coops clean, as filth is the very best place for breeding lice.

You can not breed Bantam chicks and lice in the same place and at the same time. If you doubt this, give a loosy hen a nice brood of little chicks and see the result. After one practical lesson of this kind the most skeptical will be willing to go to a great deal of trouble to keep his chicks free from vermin.

GAPES.

This is an affection seen only in young chicks from the third week to about the third month. It is, fortunately, not common in moderate climates, although said to be quite prevalent in the south.

Gapes is caused by the presence in the wind-pipe of one or more thread-like worms. These little worms attach themselves to the lining membrane of the wind-pipe and cause it to swell so that it fills the whole caliber of the pipe and the chick dies from suffocation. The principal symptom is gaping. The chick stretches his neck and opens his mouth to its fullest extent. He does this repeatedly and soon refuses to eat, becomes dumpish, and, if not relieved, dies. The only preventive is absolute cleanliness about the coops and yards.

The treatment of gapes is not very satisfactory. It consists in removing the worms from the wind-pipe. This can be accomplished by means of an instrument known as the gape worm extractor. The operation requires some skill and more patience. When a large number have to be treated the treatment is wholesale, so to speak, and the usual method is to smoke the worms out. The chicks are shut in a tight box, which is then filled with the fumes of burning sulphur or carbolic acid, or with finely powdered slacked lime. The trouble with this method is that the worms will stand about as much as the chicks will, and you will be very lucky if you can stop at just the right moment, that is, when the worms are killed and before the chicks are. Chickens that have had gapes are feeble and debilitated for a long time, and perhaps you will be more lucky, on the whole, if your smoke kills both chicks and worms.

Better direct your energies to stopping the spread of gapes than to doctoring those already affected. Take all the sick and place them in a clean, dry coop, with sand and air-slacked lime on the floor. Take the rest of the brood and all the chicks that have had access to the same yard, put them into quarters by themselves and watch very sharply, so as to remove each one to the hospital coop as soon as it shows a symptom. Be sure that any chicks that have not been exposed to danger are kept away from the infected yard, from the quarantined chicks, and, of course, from the sick ones, until the disease is thoroughly stamped out.

The infected coops and yards must be disinfected. A good way to do this is as follows: Burn all old coops that are not of much value; mix a hogshead of corrosive sublimate of strength 1 to 2000; heat to boiling point enough of this solution to saturate every part of the coops. Sprinkle the rest of the solution over the ground. When the coops are dry give a good coat of whitewash. Sprinkle air-slacked lime over the ground until no earth can be seen. Leave alone for two weeks and then spade and sow down to grass. Put no chicks into this yard for two years. Fowl may be kept in it after the grass is grown, if necessary, but no chicks.

PIP.

This is a disease of young chickens and is practically a cold. It occurs oftenest in chicks whose parents have had roup, or have been inbred too much. It is sometimes caused by damp and filthy coops.

Treatment: Give dry, clean quarters, and wash mouth and nostrils with a weak solution of chlorate of potash.

CHICKEN POX.

This is a highly contagious disease which affects both old and young. It is rather rare. It is characterized by black, hard warts or growths on the head and face.

The only treatment is to quarantine and keep the warts greased well with carbolized vaseline. Fowls will generally recover and be as good as ever, while chicks almost always succumb within a week or two after they are taken.

GOING LIGHT.

This is not a very definite term, and the condition to which it is applied is also called consumption, scrofula, congestion of the liver and inflammation. It occurs occasionally in flocks that have the best of care, so it seems there is no sure way to prevent it.

It is undoubtedly a disease of digestive organs, possibly the liver. Autopsies often show a liver rather too large, but no other abnormal condition visible to the naked eye. The symptoms are great emaciation, extreme palor of the face and comb, ruffling of feathers and general dumpishness. During the first of it the appetite is fairly good, but later disappears entirely.

When the disease attacks a chicken that is getting its second feathers, as it often does, it is, as a rule, fatal. To be of any avail treatment must be begun very early. Give sulphate of strychnine, $\frac{1}{24}$ grain, three times a day, and color the drinking water with tincture of cloride of iron. Feed meat, green food and some cooked food, as bread or mash.

When the patient is a grown fowl the treatment is somewhat different. Shut in a coop with clean sand on the floor, give calomel, $\frac{1}{4}$ grain, every two hours for five times, and no food of any kind, but plenty of water. The next morning, after these five doses, the droppings should be found in the sand, abundant and rather loose; if they are not, give a level teaspoonful of Epsom salts. After the bird has been well physicked in this way begin to feed soft food rather sparingly until your patient seems really hungry. Give the strychnine and iron, as in the previous case. As soon as the appetite returns put her back in the run where she can get more exercise and variety of food. Watch her carefully and if she grows worse again repeat the former treatment of calomel. It is often necessary to do this three or four times before thorough recovery takes place.

Now in conclusion, just a word. Remember that you will be well repaid for all the time and pains which you care to spend in giving your Bantams all proper care to keep them in good health. On the contrary, in nursing sick Bantams, your time will be frequently thrown away. The moral of this is: Do your best to prevent disease, and when it does appear, as it sometimes will in spite of your best endeavors, do not be afraid to use the hatchet.

INDEX.

Aseel Bantams	15	Gapes		44
Best Time for Hatching	8	Going Light		44
Black Breasted Red Game Bantams	11, 15	Housing Bantams		7
Brown Red Game Bantams	12, 16	Introduction		5
Birchen Game Bantams	12	Indian Game Bantams		15
Booted Bantams	23	Japanese Bantams		34
Brahma Bantams	25	Light Brahma Bantams		27
Buff Brahma Bantams	25	Leg Weakness		43
Buff Cochin Bantams	29	Lice		43
Black Cochin Bantams	30, 32	Mating		8
Burmese Bantams	39	Malay Bantams		14
Black Spanish Bantams	39	Nankin Bantams		37
Black Langshan Bantams	39	New Bantams		39
Care and Management of Bantams	8	Pyle Wheaton Hen		15
Cuckoo Cochin Bantams	30	Pekin or Cochin Bantams		28
Cuckoo Bantams	37	Partridge Cochin Bantams		31
Care of Bantams	32	Polish Bantams		38
Cold	41	Preparing for Exhibition		40
Canker or Diphtheritic Roup	42	Pip		44
Cholera	42	Red Pyle Bantams		14
Crop Bound	42	Red Wheaton Hen		15
Chicken Pox	44	Red Pyle Game Bantams		15
Dark Brahma Bantams	27	Rose Comb Bantams		21
Duckwing Bantams	15	Roup		41, 42
Duckwing Wheaton Hen	15	Size and Weight		8
Double Mating	28	Starving Bantams—A Wrong Idea		9
Diseases of Bantams	41	Silver Duckwing Game Bantams		16
Diarrhea	42	Sebright Bantams		17
Food and Feeding	7	Sultan Bantams		24
Food and Water	9	Sultan or Booted White Polish		38
From Secretary National Bantam Association	33	Silky Bantams		38
		Scaly Bantams		43
Frizzled and Rumpless Bantams	36	White and Black Bantams		14
Game Bantams	10	White Cochin Bantams		31
Golden Duckwing Bantams	16	Washing Birds for Exhibition		40

DIRECTORY OF BANTAM BREEDERS.

P. H. FRELINGHUYSEN, Morristown, New Jersey.

KELLY BROS., Norfolk, Virginia.

A. E. BLUNCK, Johnstown, N. Y., breeder and importer of all varieties of Game and Ornamental Bantams. Winners at New York, Boston, Kansas City and other leading shows.

A. N. MASTERSON, 278 Baker Street, Detroit, Mich., breeds Black Tailed Japanese, Buff and Partridge Cochin Bantams of the finest quality. Good stock always for sale.

ARTHUR PORTER, Galena, Ill., breeds Buff Cochin Bantams exclusively. Quality, not quantity, is his motto. Eggs from selected matings, $2 per sitting. Stock and eggs in season. Correspondence solicited.

A. L. CUTTING, Weston, Mass. Cutting's Bantams, bred in closer, have won hundreds of prizes. Typical Rose Comb Blacks and wonderful Cochin shape. Buff Cochin Bantams are my specialties.

FRED CROSBY, Seaton, Ill., breeds Buff Cochin Bantams that win prizes. Six first prizes on five birds at the great Moline show. Have sold stock that won at other shows in strong competition. Stock for sale.

W. C. CAPEN, 210 Washington Avenue, St. Louis, Mo., has for sale Buff Cochin Bantams. Thoroughbreds. No eggs. No circulars.

S. A. NOFTZGER, North Manchester, Ind. When wanting anything extra good in B. R. Red Game Bantam fowls, chicks or eggs, write me. I have bred from three of America's best prize this year.

W. W. CLOUGH, Medway, Mass., owner of New England's largest Bantam yards. Circulars free.

J. B. NEVIUS, 483 Provident Building, Philadelphia, Pa., importer and breeder of Buff, Black and White Cochin Bantams, White, Black and Gray Japanese Bantams.

DAVID B. HUFFMAN, Box 32, Nashville, Ill., breeds Rose Comb Black Bantams. His breeders are all Canadian or Madison Square winners. Eggs, $2.50 per 13. Stock according to merit.

W. ROBERT DUNLOP, Box 34, Fayetteville, N. Y., breeder of S. C. Brown Leghorns. A limited number of sittings from first-class birds, noted to produce high class specimens. Circular free.

DR. B. BRUST, New Albany, Ind., breeder of Buff Cochin Bantams (McGrew and Dr Fox strains), Silver Spangled Hamburgs, Golden Pheasants, high class English Carriers, Nellieettes, Bloodmittes, Jacobins and Archangels.

CHARLES JEMS, Elberon, N. J., winner at New York of thirty-one prizes, twenty specials, three cups and medals. Birds for sale at $5 per pair in the following varieties: Black Red, Brown Red and Red Pyle Game Bantams, and Black, White and Buff Cochin Bantams.

W. M. CLARKE, Brookfield, N. Y., breeder of Black Red and Brown Red Games, and Black Red and Red Pyle Game Bantams. Birds from my yards, in my own and customers' hands have won first honors at all the leading eastern shows in this country. A few good birds always for sale.

M. MAYER, P. O. Box 125, Brunswick, Ga., breeds high class B. C Bantams. G. S. Bantams, Partridge Cochins, W. C. Black Polish and Barred Plymouth Rocks. Write for prices.

M. C. SADEWATER, Belvidere, Ill., breeder of White and Buff Cochin Bantams, fine in standard requirements. Prices low. Stock guaranteed to satisfy.

SMITH CURREY, West Chester, Pa., breeder of the "Golden Rod" strain of Buff Cochin Bantams. Eggs from my prize winning yards, $3 per 13. Breeders and exhibition stock for sale at all times.

DR. WILLIAM Y. FOX, Taunton, Mass. White, Black and Buff Cochin Bantams. I breed Bantams that win at Boston and New York shows, and I sell good stock cheap.

W. H. BOGART, 11 Amherst St., East Orange, N. J., breeder of Golden and Silver Sebrights. A few choice sittings of eggs for sale this season.

THE SOUTH SIDE POULTRY YARDS, 319 Walker St., Milwaukee, Wis., breeders of Buff Cochins and Cochin Bantams. Fowls and eggs for sale at all seasons of the year.

JOHN M. LUCKENBILL, 123 So. 16th St., Reading, Pa., breeds Buff Cochin Bantams and White Wyandottes up-to-date in size, shape and color. Stock and eggs for sale.

CHARLES C. MUNROE, 287 Cedar St., New Bedford, Mass., has sold his Bantams, but has high class Magpies for sale. Fancy Mice a specialty.

J. W. MULINIX, 649 South Erie St., Toledo, Ohio, breeder of America's best B. B. R. Game Bantams and Black Rose Combs.

ALBERT W. LEWIS, Fall River, Mass., proprietor of Lakeside Poultry Yards, breeder of Black Cochins. Winnings on application. Good stock always for sale. Eggs, $5 per 13.

THE BROOK RANCH, Salt Lake City, Utah, has for sale some fine Bantam fowls. They will take good care of all orders.

DAVID A. NICHOLS, Monroe, Conn., breeder of first-class Black Cochin Bantams. Write for prices.

CLARENCE HENDERSON, Springfield, Ohio, proprietor "Buckeye Poultry Yards," breeds high grade Buff Cochin Bantams. Write for prices.

M. M. FULLARTON, Leonia, N. J., breeder of Dark Brahmas and Partridge Cox. Pit Bantams. First-class stock for sale. Write.

PRITCHARD & EMERSON, Weston, Mass., breeders of Games and Bantams of all varieties. Write me what you need. Prompt attention given all inquiries.

S. B. FERRELL, Granbury, Texas, breeds twelve varieties of Bantams strictly up-to-date, and winners in six states. Stock and eggs for sale. Circulars free.

W. W. CONGDON, Oak Lawn, R. I., Black, White, Buff and Partridge Cochin, Bearded and White White Polish, White Booted and Light Brahma Bantams. Eggs and stock for sale.

COL. JOSEPH LEFFEL, Springfield, Ohio, is the most extensive breeder of poultry and pets in America. Rabbits, Guinea Pigs, Ferrets, Pigeons, Dogs, Maltese Cats, Shetland Ponies. Circulars free.

JOHN C. KIRKPATRICK, Easton, Pa., breeder of Buff and Black Cochin Bantams. Have purchased from Long Acre Farm the second Boston Black cockerel, also the second Bantam Buff cock. With such grand birds heading my pens I claim the equal of any breeder in this country. Stock and eggs for sale at reasonable prices.

G. DALE McCLASKEY, Papillion, Neb., breeds the choicest of exhibition Buff Cochin Bantams. Stock and eggs in season.

JOHN BASS, Newark, N. J. If you want something odd and beautiful, buy White Silky Bantams. Stock and eggs at reasonable prices.

CHARLES C. REISS, 12th and Elm, Reading, Pa., breeder exhibition B. B. Red, Red Pyle and Buff Pekin Bantams. Babcock, Mohan and Myers strains respectively.

WOODCLEFT POULTRY YARDS, Freeport, N. Y. New York, Boston and Washington winners. Buff, White, Black Cochins, Black Red, Red Pyle and Silver Duckwing Game Bantams.

MRS. W. PECK, Cedar Point, Kan., breeder Buff Cochin Bantams. Breeding and exhibition stock for sale. Nothing but scored birds offered. Eggs, $2.50 for 10.

E. L. FREEMAN, East Millstone, N. J., breeder of Buff, White and Black Cochin Bantams. Breeding stock reasonable prices. No stock for sale till fall 1899.

IRA C. KELLER, Prospect, Ohio, breeder and importer of Golden and Silver Sebrights for twenty-five years. Winners at World's Fair, New York and Bantam Club show.

JAMES HALLENBECK, Altamont, N. Y., breeder silver Sebright, Buff Cochin, Black Red Game Bantams. Also Barred Rocks, Buff and White Leghorns. All of the finest.

"ZUM," Gloversville, N. Y. Silver and Golden Sebrights, Black and White Cochin. Bearded and non-bearded White Polish, Black Red Game Bantams; English Beagle Hounds.

THOMAS PARKER, Johnstown, N. Y., breeder of exhibition Bantams. Black Reds, Brown Reds, Duckwings, Pyles, Birchens, White Game, Golden and Silver Sebrights, White and Buff Cochins.

EDWARD LYNCH, S. 1326 Minnehaha St., Rondine, St. Paul, Minn., breeder of White Crested White Polish and Pekin Bantams, and Black Tailed Japanese.

RANSOM JONES, Penn Yan, N. Y., breeder of White Game and Buff Cochin Bantams. Eggs and stock for sale. Satisfaction guaranteed.

J. B. WEBB, DeWitt, Iowa, breeder of Golden Sebright, White and Black Cochin Bantams. Stock for sale. Eggs, $2 for 13. Express prepaid on eggs.

WM. McNEIL, London, Ontario, Canada. For sale, White and Buff Cochins, Golden and Silver Sebrights, Black Rose Combs, all varieties of Japanese and Polish, Japanese Silkies.

ALEX. VAN WYCK, New Whatcom, Wash., breeder of Buff Cochin Bantams, from the best blood in the country.

G. F. SOUTHWICK, Beloit, Wis., breeder Black Minorcas, Black Africans, Golden Sebrights, White, Black, Buff Cochin Bantams, Peruvian and common Guinea Pigs. Eggs and stock in season.

B. F. SIMONDS, Garden City, Kan., breeder of the best strains of following Bantams: Buff, White, Black Cochin Bantams, Black Breasted Red, Red Pyle and Silver Duckwing Game Bantams. Eggs, $2 per 13.

A. FORNEY, Elwood, Ind., breeder of the choicest B. B. Reds, S. D. Wings, R. Pyle Games, Silver Sebrights, Buff Pekin Bantams. Stock for sale. Eggs in season.

EMIL G. RAASCH, 319 Walker Street, Milwaukee, Wis., breeder of Buff, Black, White and Partridge Cochin Bantams. Stock and eggs for sale. Satisfaction guaranteed.

LYNEHURST POULTRY YARDS, Glassboro, N. J., breeders of high class Cochins, Cochin and Japanese Bantams. Exhibition and breeding birds for sale. Eggs in season. Office, 483 Provident Building, Philadelphia, Pa.

DIRECTORY OF BANTAM BREEDERS Continued

JOHN BAUSCHER, Jr., Freeport, Ill. Box 222. Choice Buff Cochin, Golden Sebright and Black Tail Japanese Bantams for sale. Send 15c for large, eighty-page book, explains all.

STEM BROS., Easton, Pa., Midget Bantam Yards. Buff and Black Cochin Bantams. Winners Mt. Gretna, Hagerstown, Trenton, Waverly and Allentown. Stock and eggs for sale.

CHARLES M. SMITH, 161 Crystal Street, Brooklyn, N. Y. Prize winning Buff and White Cochin, Black Rose Comb Bantams. Eggs, $2 per 13. Stock in season.

A. C. TOMB, Eureka, Ill., breeder of Bantams that are winners. Buff and White Cochin Bantams. Stock for sale at reasonable prices. Eggs in season.

E. R. SPAULDING, Jaffrey, N. H., breeder of M. B. Red and Game Bantams; twenty-five years experience. We breed and sell birds that win at best shows.

G. A. C. CLARKE, Le Mars, Iowa, breeder of P. B. R. Game Bantams. Birds are extra, both in shape and color. Breeding stock at reasonable prices. Also exhibition birds.

HUGH C. BEELMAN, 833 Warren Avenue, Chicago, Ill., breeder of Golden Sebrights exclusively. Quality right, prices reasonable. Stock birds cheap to make room.

L. L. LUCAS, Oil City, Pa., breeder of Gold Strain Buff Cochin Bantams. Prices from $1 up. Stock for sale at all times. Satisfaction guaranteed.

PHILANDER WILLIAMS, Taunton Mass., breeder of Buff and Black Cochin Bantams and Golden Sebright Bantams. Have bred the Sebrights for thirty years. Stock for sale.

W. T. NAYLOR, Painesville, Ohio, breeder of prize Buff Cochin Bantams. Birds small and of the best strains in America. Stock for sale. Eggs in season.

CLIFFORD GOTT, Horsforth, Leeds, England, originator of Cornish Indian Game Bantams, the new and fast becoming variety of Bantams. Winners at all best English shows. Latest, two firsts, second, third, Birmingham; two firsts, medal, special, second, Leeds. Also Silver Sebright, Frizzle, Rose Comb, Pekin, and Old English Game Bantams. Commissions executed. Highest references. Stamp for reply.

C. E. ROCKENSTYRE, Albany, N. Y., twenty years as importer, breeder and judge of all standard varieties of Bantams. Only the best kept or sold.

J. B. VOSS, Davenport, Iowa, breeder of the pure Ainsworth Black Red Game Bantams. Best is cheapest in the end. Try our birds or eggs.

MRS. E. HOLLARD, Highland, Ill. Bargains in Buff Cochin Bantams bred from birds that are true bred and pure blooded, if taken soon, 25c to $2 each. First-class stock.

WILLIAM M. HUGHES, South Portsmouth, R. I., twenty years a breeder thoroughbred fowls. Black Langshans. Originator of Black Langshan Bantams. No eggs for sale.

D. LINCOLN ORR, Orr's Mills, N. Y., importer and breeder of Light and Dark Brahma Bantams. Elegant little fellows that will please. No eggs.

E. LATHAM, Fishbush, Long Island, N. Y. Golden Rod strain Buff Cochin Bantams, bred to successfully compete with America's choicest specimens. Fancy birds, reasonable prices.

M. J. BUNDY, Tustin, Orange County, Cal., breeder of several breeds of Bantams. Correspondence solicited.

E. HENRY GALUSHA, 229 Water St., Allentown, Pa., breeder of high class exhibition, ornamental Bantams. Highest honors at America's largest shows. Correspondence solicited.

JOHN MELVIN, Whitinsville, Mass., breeder Black B. Red and Pyle Red Game, Black and White Rose Comb and Sebright Bantams. My breeding stock is imported.

CHARLES T. CORNMAN, Carlisle, Pa., breeds all varieties of America's best Games, Game and variety Bantams. If you do not believe it, look up the awards of the great shows. Eggs in season. Stock for sale. Send for price card.

WILLIAM H. MACHOLDT, 1167 Myrtle Ave., near Broadway, Brooklyn, N. Y., breeder Buff Cochin Bantams. Birds small, well feathered. Color eggs for sale in season.

IRVIN S. MILLER, 147 Chew St., Allentown, Pa., breeder of Bantams, all varieties. Japanese, Golden and Silver Sebrights, Black Rose Comb, Bearded, White Crested Polish Bantams.

GEORGE G. ROSE, Shawneetown, Ill., proprietor White Rose Poultry Farm. Bantams. Beauties and winners. Black Cochin, Black Red Games, Buff Cochin, Red Pyle Games, White Cochins, Bearded and Crested White Polish. Eggs and stock in season.

B. C. THORNTON, South Vineland, N. J., breeder and importer of all varieties of Game Bantams. Highest type of exhibition birds a specialty.

S. D. DRURY, Northampton, Mass., breeds Golden Sebrights only for love of excellence in the breed, not for the profits in the business.

www.ingramcontent.com/pod-product-compliance
Lightning Source LLC
Chambersburg PA
CBHW030709110426
42739CB00031B/1520